Lost at 40

Finding Purpose and Joy After Forty

VARUNA PATHAK

INDIA • SINGAPORE • MALAYSIA

ISBN
Paperback 979-8-89556-843-9
Hardcase 979-8-89632-415-7

CONTENTS

Chapter 1

INTRODUCTION: AWAKENING AT MIDLIFE

"The greatest fear in the world is of the opinions of others. And the moment you are unafraid of the crowd, you are no longer a sheep; you become a lion. A great roar arises in your heart, the roar of freedom."

— Osho

In the autumn of 2023, a persistent thought began to echo in my mind. I couldn't pinpoint why, but it nudged me to reassess the life I had lived so far. Like many of you, this period of introspection coincided with the hormonal shifts of menopause, setting the stage for profound internal changes. The common narrative suggests that life is halfway over at this point, but I was not ready to accept that. Instead, I saw it as a chance for a fresh start.

As a young girl, I was exceptionally obedient, always doing as I was told, rewarded for following rules and being a "good girl". This compliance served me well at home and in school, but as I stepped into the broader world, it faltered. I found myself constantly adjusting to fit moulds set by others based on years of conditioning. As I stood on the threshold of fifty, I realised it was time to start listening to myself — to redefine who I was beyond the instructions and expectations placed upon me. It was as if all the wires, the connections, the pathways in my software were entangled, and the system had crashed. Where was I? Who was I? What was I searching for? I was not here to give you labels like midlife or menopause. I'm here to share that if you're looking for ready-made solutions to the chaos in your head, you might be disappointed. But know that you're not alone. Welcome aboard; join the club of those who've taken the time to realise what went wrong.

What's gone is gone. You were good, and you still are, and you will continue to be. But the definitions will change, as will the judging parameters. Now, only you will judge yourself. Why? Because your madness, your unique reactions and treatments of solutions define you. If you start following someone else's script, you'll lose yourself. Don't give up your uniqueness. It's what makes you different. Imagine if elephants decided to mimic the gait of horses; it wouldn't work. Similarly, if you let others impose their styles and methods on you, you will fail disastrously. These are not just trivial choices. These small everyday decisions define you. By midlife, you realise how important it is to stick to your own colours and not let others use you as their canvas. Being stretched too far is painfully unbearable, and wounds from those close are hard to heal. Set your boundaries before it's too late.

As we consider the shifts that come with age, let me tell you about a vivid memory of my last trip before the world came to a standstill with COVID. I went on a trek to the Valley of Flowers in the Himalayas. At forty-five, I wasn't the athletic type, and the thirteen-kilometre trek from Joshimath to Ghagaria was daunting. There were easier options (helicopters, horses), but choosing them would mean missing the essence of the journey through the breathtaking Himalayan landscapes.

Reflecting on that journey from the comfort of home, I recognised it was more than reaching a scenic valley. This journey symbolised the effort, the grit required to traverse those paths. The most profound lesson I learned was the importance of taking that first step. Amidst physical exhaustion and scarce breath, it wasn't just about endurance but mental resilience. Just lift one leg, and suddenly, you've moved forward. That uncertain, shaky first step teaches you that as long as you can lift your leg, you can face anything. It's about moving forward, one step at a time.

As the day faded during my trek, the dimming sky paralleled my own fatigue, each signalling a pause, a moment to gather strength for the days ahead. The next day was filled with possibilities, like waiting for the next part of a film after an intermission, eager and anticipative of what was to come. This journey underscored the power of small, determined actions and how a single step can lead to another, forging a path forward through sheer will, even when the end seems nowhere in sight. It's a testament to the human spirit's ability to overcome and ascend beyond physical realms, reaching into mental and emotional endurance.

So, as you reflect on your own life's journey, slowly prepare yourself to take that first step, to push through the doubts and fears. It's not just about reaching the pinnacle but about embracing the journey, learning from each step, and growing stronger with every challenge. This is the essence of living – not merely surviving but thriving by continually striving for greatness, however you define it, one step at a time.

However, starting anew means preparing for the journey ahead. You don't pack everything you own; you choose what's essential and leave behind what's not. Are you ready to shift gears at any moment in your life? The life you're living now, with all its routines and certainties, is the only certain thing you have. If there are other paths you yearn to explore, dreams you've yet to chase that seem within reach, then why hesitate? Life offers no guarantees of a tomorrow to pursue those dreams. **It's time to change gears now while you still have the time, resources, and energy to enjoy what might come next.**

How often have you considered the daunting prospect of ending up on your deathbed filled with regrets for not having lived differently? Remember, no situation is permanently perfect or disastrous; much of how we fare is shaped by our own capabilities and personality. You're likely to flourish wherever you find yourself, thanks to your inherent qualities. Changing your path should not be a source of fear. Driven by your inner resilience, you're unlikely to fall below your current level. In fact, there's a good chance things will only improve.

Having served in a government job for almost twenty years, I used to feel I was not happy, nor was my family ever happy with that job. I worked under immense pressure and wasn't able to attain the work-life balance I needed. Even my friends in the sector pushed me to look for better opportunities. However, I used to stay put, enticed by the security of my job. I was honestly sceptical about whether I would be able to generate the same revenue as my secured salary. So, when I finally took the leap and resigned, the one big thing I realised after quitting was that at all times, I was the one ensuring that every day was more rewarding than the last. And that feeling of independent growth is highly reassuring and worth it all—unless, of course, you become physically or mentally incapable.

Your health and vitality are your true wealth. As long as you're alive and capable, you can make things happen. You are the anchor that prevents your life from dipping below a certain standard. Don't fret over potential failures; instead, focus on the heights you could reach. Remember, people won't recall your failures; they'll celebrate your successes. Think about those who finally pass challenging exams after multiple attempts; once they succeed, their past struggles are overshadowed by their achievement. Embrace failure as part of your journey; don't let it mire you in self-pity.

If you look at the animals in the wild, they face daily threats yet continue to thrive without letting fear paralyse them. If they don't let the fear of failure or death deter them, why should we? As we age, achieving our goals doesn't mean we settle. That same ambition that drove us to early successes keeps us striving for more. This relentless pursuit might sometimes leave us feeling unsatisfied, but it also drives us to continue contributing, perhaps by mentoring others or taking on less demanding roles that still allow us to utilise our skills effectively.

So, are you ready to reevaluate your path, to embrace the chance of a new direction in your life? For those who have been merely floating, now might be the time to start questioning. It's not too late to change some aspects of your life and ensure you live on your terms. If you relinquish control of your life to others, your needs might become secondary. Let's explore what it means to truly listen to oneself, to challenge lifelong conditioning, and to embrace transformation at any age. We won't just look back or ponder what-ifs. We'll look forward, armed with the lessons of the past and the courage to forge new paths. Together, we will discover that **it's never too late to reshape our lives and redefine our destinies**. As you turn these pages, I invite you to join me in redefining what midlife means.

Chapter 2

WHY YOU NEED TO BUILD YOUR OWN HAPPINESS

"You feel good, you feel bad, and these feelings are bubbling from your own unconsciousness, from your own past. Nobody is responsible except you. Nobody can make you angry, and nobody can make you happy."

— Osho

Reflect back to your earliest memories — were you ever just two or four years old, playing without a care with your siblings or toddler friends? Back then, we didn't know about our genders, social positions, or religions. The world was simple; it revolved around exploration, appreciation, and the sheer joy of receiving little things for our tiny bodies and curious minds. Remember how, in those moments, we all believed in equal opportunities? We were democrats of our tiny worlds, limitless until someone told us otherwise. Even as we grew and life began to carve out our distinct niches, that sense of boundless possibility lingered.

Can you still recall that laughter? That uninhibited dance? The way we could cry so openly or fall without fear? That was our truest self — free and unabashedly happy. It's hard to deny, isn't it?

For those who have settled into the role of "doing the maximum we could," deep down, you remember what pure happiness feels like because you've tasted it. If you veer away from that happiness, a part of you will always know what you've missed, and that realisation might someday grip you with a profound sense of loss. Why not close that gap for yourself now?

I often meet people in their midlives who criticise the dream chasers. They portray themselves as the more content type, the moderates at peace because they've reconciled with their circumstances. They've stopped dreaming, believing that to dream was to harm both themselves and their loved ones. But now, it's time to ask, "You've prioritised everyone else over you. Now, isn't it time to revive those dreams?"

By this age, your wisdom should help you see things, people, and relationships more clearly. It's as though life's report cards are finally out, revealing the true nature of every interaction and every investment of effort and emotion. Many of you out there have lived a life trying to please your in-laws for almost two plus decades, trying to prove to them that you are a good human being, that your intentions towards family are selfless and that you are thoroughly efficient in running the household. You've been trying to prove your worth. And, yes, in almost all families, your in-laws have definitely recognised your capabilities and have also realised your indispensable position in the extended and immediate family. But in families where this has not happened even now, what miracle do you think is about to happen which will now change your position from that of an outsider to a family member? This is a point to ponder on. Suddenly, it becomes clear who is who and what is what. You know by now who is on your side and who is not. With this clarity, your own worth begins to crystallise. **You realise what you could have achieved, what you were truly capable of if only you had acted or, perhaps more accurately, been allowed to act.**

Finding joy in others' happiness and stepping back to let loved ones grow can indeed be fulfilling if it's genuinely for the greater good. But must it always come at the expense of your own dreams? Every time you give up a piece of your pie, the next time, not only will they not offer you a slice, but they may not even recognise your sacrifice. Worse, you teach them to expect your selflessness as a given. This isn't just about you; it's about the example you set for your children or those under your influence. By playing the martyr, you risk teaching them to be insensitive to others, perpetuating emotional neglect across generations.

I'm not advocating for selfishness or self-centredness. Instead, I urge you to live a fair life. While sacrifices for the greater good are noble, they should not always come at your expense. True victory isn't about individual wins but when the team triumphs. But for a team to truly win, the pie must be divided equally. Happiness in any unit, be it family or work, depends on this balance of give and take. When I say the pie should be divided equally, I mean responsibilities must be shared fairly, too. To receive fairly, one must contribute fairly. Let's strive for a life where everyone's contributions and rewards are balanced and happiness is truly shared. Isn't it about time?

SOCIETAL INFLUENCES ON HAPPINESS

As we begin this journey together, let's begin by questioning the very fabric of our societal constructs. Ever wonder who authors the scripts of our lives and why we adhere to them so faithfully?

Our understanding of happiness often starts to take shape right from childhood, doesn't it? Fairy tales, movies, and advertisements craft a picture of what life should be, of the certain milestones filled with a lucrative job, a loving spouse, children, and a home straight out of a magazine. But have you noticed? These are not just stories or goals; they become societal metrics for measuring our success and happiness. How often have we found ourselves striving not for what truly brings joy but for what garners approval and applause from others? This dilemma is particularly pronounced in the Indian context, where collective societal approval often outweighs personal satisfaction, steering us away from what might genuinely fulfil us.

In India, the pursuit of economic stability is often seen as the ultimate goal, isn't it? This quest can lead us down a path of relentless striving, where our careers and financial achievements are deemed the primary indicators of a successful life. But at what cost? The cultural scene of

India also comes with its own set of expectations – marriage at a 'suitable' age, children, and adherence to traditional roles. These norms can become stifling cages that constrain our personal growth. How many of us have forgone passions or careers that didn't align with these societal blueprints? It's essential we introspect and dissect how these economic and cultural pressures not only shape our decisions but also how stepping away from them might lead us to more authentic happiness.

The intersection of gender roles and societal expectations paints a complex picture in India. Despite progress towards gender equality, traditional roles often dictate that women prioritise family over personal ambitions. Many women find themselves as the primary caregivers, managing the complexities of home while their personal aspirations take a backseat. But why should growth and opportunity be limited by gender? If a woman possesses the skills and the drive to assume roles traditionally held by men, embracing these opportunities can lead to a more fulfilling life. **It's not about individual success; true victory is when every member of the family, or team, thrives together.**

In exploring these areas, we aim not just to identify the challenges but also to forge pathways to overcome them. It's about recognising the external pressures for what they are and daring to redefine our criteria for happiness. Let's take this step together, understanding these influences, and finding ways to assert our own narratives and begin the journey towards a happiness that is truly your own.

REDEFINING MIDLIFE

Midlife is often seen through a lens of dread, portrayed as a time of crisis or turmoil. But what if we saw it not as a crisis but as a pivotal opportunity for personal growth and reawakening? In the Indian context, where societal and familial expectations weigh heavily, midlife presents a unique chance to reassess and revitalise our lives' paths.

Isn't it interesting that midlife often arrives just as we feel settled in our ways? For many Indian women, this stage becomes a turning point to reevaluate what truly matters. After years of fulfilling roles determined by others (whether as dedicated daughters, caring mothers, or devoted wives), midlife offers a quieter moment to turn down the volume of external expectations. It's a chance to ask ourselves: Are we living a life that's true to our inner desires, or are we just ticking boxes set by others? This period of life invites us to rediscover passions long shelved to meet the urgent demands of earlier decades. Perhaps you once dreamt of painting, writing, or starting your own business. Now could be the time to pick up where you left off or to discover new interests that resonate with your current self. It's a moment to rekindle old dreams or ignite new ones, stepping into roles that fulfil us beyond traditional expectations. Also, why I say this is because many of you may be about to go through an empty nest phase. Another rule that operates is that for any venture to take shape, you should ideally have started working on it for 4-5 years. So, start working on it before you get gripped by the dreaded empty nest syndrome.

The narrative of the 'midlife crisis' is in desperate need of an overhaul. We often hear about the downsides, the lost opportunities and confusion about the future. Yet, is this stage not also ripe with possibilities? Consider it a second spring, where life can flourish in new, enriching ways. In India, where one's life path is often heavily influenced by extended family and societal duties, questioning and challenging these myths can lead to a liberating redefinition of midlife. How can you transform this supposed crisis into a catalyst for empowerment and rejuvenation? It's about viewing this phase not as the sunset of your youth but as the dawn of a new era filled with opportunities to learn, grow, and contribute in ways that are meaningful to you.

There's immense power in stories, especially those of women who have transformed their midlife uncertainties into periods of triumph. These stories often involve stepping out from under the long shadows of conventional roles to claim a life rich with personal achievements and satisfaction. From pursuing delayed passions like art or education to switching careers or starting new ventures, these narratives are inspiring and transformative. In your own community, there may be women whose lives mirror these tales of courage and change. Or perhaps you find yourself on the brink of such a transformation. Sharing these stories can light the path for others in similar situations and cultivate a community of support and encouragement.

Let's reimagine midlife as a vibrant chapter of our lives, not a crisis to be managed but an exciting stage to be enjoyed and savoured. It's not about fading into the background as we age but stepping into the spotlight of our own lives with confidence and joy. What stories will you write in this renewed phase of your journey? How will you celebrate and redefine midlife as a period of personal renaissance and unexpected adventures?

BUILDING PERSONAL HAPPINESS

In the pursuit of happiness, it's tempting to mirror the paths others have taken, to adopt their manners and mimic their lifestyles. But have you ever paused to consider whether these adopted personas truly fit you, or are you just trying to fill a role that society has scripted for you? Life, vast and intricate, is also compact and fleeting. Wearing someone else's identity can't sustain us for long. It's like wearing clothes that don't fit. Eventually, they become uncomfortable.

How often do you manage your behaviour to align with others' expectations at work, at home, or in social settings? Reflect on this: pretending to be someone you're not can lead to deep-seated unhappiness. The human psyche is complex, with every action and reaction intertwined. For instance, adopting a soft-spoken demeanour might seem appealing, but if it isn't paired with genuine kindness, won't people see through it? If you're only acting out of self-interest but cloak your actions in sweetness, you might be perceived as manipulative. That's why **it's essential to be true to yourself. Discover what fuels you to affirm who you really are.**

Believe in yourself. Accepting who you truly are is the first step towards genuine happiness. Are you setting goals based on what truly matters to you, or are you chasing benchmarks set by others? It's crucial to align your aspirations with your true nature. Even if your nature leans towards self-interest, owning it without pretence is healthier than wearing a mask of generosity. Authenticity breeds contentment, so set goals that reflect your true self, not an image crafted for someone else's approval.

As we journey towards genuine self-acceptance and happiness, it's crucial to employ various introspective techniques that help us align our external lives with our internal truths. Consider journalling. More than a structured exercise, it's also a free-form way to express your thoughts and feelings. This can be a powerful tool for self-discovery, helping you articulate and confront the realities of who you are versus who you think you should be.

Beyond journalling, simply taking time for deep introspection can be invaluable. This might involve reflecting during quiet moments, perhaps while walking or sitting in a peaceful setting, allowing your thoughts to flow naturally and seeing where they lead. If self-guided introspection feels daunting, seeking external help can be beneficial. A therapist or a trusted mentor can offer guidance and a fresh perspective, helping you navigate through your thoughts and feelings about authenticity and happiness.

These non-prescriptive, flexible approaches allow you to explore your identity and desires at your own pace. They are gentle reminders that understanding oneself is not about rigorous exercises but about creating space to reflect, learn, and grow in authenticity with deliberate and joyful intention. Practice these reflective practices, making a deeper connection with yourself and paving the way towards a more authentic and joyful life. Remember, if you keep changing colours to please everyone, you might end up losing yourself completely. It's about changing not for the sake of others, but for your own peace and happiness.

By building a foundation based on personal truth rather than societal expectations, we pave the way to a happiness that is not only more profound but also more enduring. Let's begin this beautiful construction project together, laying each brick with intention and joy.

TAKING ACTION

Knowing what makes us truly happy is a significant first step, but the journey doesn't end there. Real change happens through decisive, intentional action.

Remember how, as children, we lived without constraints, embracing each day with joy and boundless curiosity? Why should that sense of possibility diminish as we grow older? As we navigate midlife, many of us have shelved our dreams, settling into the comfort of routine and the familiar. But isn't it time to ask whether you are truly content or just comfortable? Being proactive means stepping out of these comfort zones, challenging the status quo, and taking responsibility for our happiness. **It's about not waiting for opportunities but creating them.** Isn't it time to revive those dreams?

Change can be as simple as deciding to spend more time on your hobbies or as significant as a career transition. Think about the dreams you've packed away. What small steps can you take today to bring them back to life? Remember, every large journey begins with a single, small step. Whether it's signing up for a painting class or planning a long-overdue vacation, start with something that reignites your passion.

And what about those dreams that require bigger shifts, like changing careers or relocating? Start by visualising where you want to be. Imagine your life in this new role or new city. What does it feel like? What are the steps you need to take to get there? While these decisions are significant, they don't have to be overwhelming. Break them down into manageable actions. Perhaps you need to enrol in a course, update your resume, or simply start saving money. Each step, no matter how small, is a step towards your new dream. It keeps you alive. It gives you a reason to get up every morning. It gives you a reason to keep yourself healthy and active. It gives you the reason to pull on your sneakers and hit the gym. It prevents you from withering away each day.

But it's not just about taking external actions. Significant changes require internal shifts too. How do you view change? Do you see it as an opportunity or a threat? Embracing change as a positive force is crucial. It's about shifting from a mindset that fears the unknown to one that sees potential and growth in every new challenge. Consider the freedoms and joys of your early childhood, when every new day was an adventure. Can you bring that sense of wonder and possibility into your adult decisions?

As you go on this journey of change, remember, it's not just about altering your external circumstances but also about transforming how you think and feel about your life. So, take that step to not just dream but actively pursue those dreams with the enthusiasm of your childhood self. The path is before you, and it's never too late to start walking it. By embracing both the need for action and the necessity of mindset shifts, you pave the way for a future that reflects your deepest desires and aspirations. Let's not wait for life to happen to us; let's craft the life we've always imagined.

CONCLUSION:

In this chapter, we discussed the influences on our happiness and how we can actively reshape and reclaim it. We started by understanding how societal expectations, economic pressures, and rigid gender roles can cloud our perception of what happiness truly means. We then challenged the myths of midlife, turning what many view as a crisis into a launchpad for personal revival and growth.

As we moved forward, we delved into the essentials of building personal happiness through self-discovery and setting personal goals. We provided practical exercises to help you dig deep and discover what truly lights up your life. Finally, we discussed the importance of taking proactive steps towards these discoveries, emphasising that change, though daunting, is necessary and ultimately rewarding.

Let me remind you: it's never too late to seek out happiness. No matter where you are in your life, no matter how set in your ways you might feel, there is always room for joy, for growth, for change. The path to happiness is built day by day, choice by choice. It's up to you to take those brave steps towards a life that fulfills you deeply and truly.

So, I urge you now: don't wait for a sign or a perfect moment. The perfect moment is now, and the sign is your own heart beating, yearning for more. Start small if you must, but start today. Reevaluate your path, set goals that resonate with you, and begin making those small shifts in your life. Each step you take is a step closer to the happiness you deserve.

Let's not just dream about a better life; let's make it happen. Together, let's build our happiness, one joyful, purposeful step at a time.

Chapter 3

PRINCIPLE 1: DREAM BOLDLY – RECLAIM YOUR DREAMS

"Every great dream begins with a dreamer. Always remember, you have within you the strength, the patience, and the passion to reach for the stars to change the world."

— Harriet Tubman

Have you ever paused, maybe while sorting through an old box of photos or cleaning out a drawer, and stumbled across the dreams you packed away years ago? Perhaps it was a sketch from your college days when you thought you'd be an artist, or maybe a business plan for that café you dreamt of opening. Here we are, well into our forties and fifties, and it seems like those dreams might just stay tucked away forever, right? Wrong.

Let's have a little chat about this. We've all been there, haven't we? Sacrificing our passions on the altar of 'being practical' or 'doing the right thing' as defined by, well, everyone but ourselves. We are all expected to be the 'good girls', the self-sacrificing martyrs society wants us to be. We followed the rules, and yes, they served us well… up to a point. But here's a thought: **maybe the rules need to change as we do.**

Why do we often treat our dreams like delicate china, only to be admired from afar and never used? Think about it. We've spent years building careers, raising families, and filling roles that were sometimes more about expectations than aspirations. And here's where it gets interesting: who says life's second act can't be as thrilling as the first, or even more so?

This chapter isn't just another pep talk. It's a nudge, a somewhat cheeky reminder that if not now, then when? Life is hardly over at fifty. Heck, it's got all the drama and excitement of a Bollywood comeback, minus the numerous dance sequences (unless, of course, you like that sort of thing). Why should the younger version of you have all the fun with dreams and daring adventures? It's time to dust off those dreams and dress them up for the life you live now, rich with the wisdom and freedom that come with being 'of a certain age.'

So, what's the game plan? First, we identify those dusty dreams. And no, it's not too late. Did you know there are plenty of people who embarked on new adventures and nailed it in their fifties and beyond? There's something incredibly empowering about picking up where you left off, whether it's resurrecting an old hobby, starting a new venture, or finally taking that dream trip to Italy.

I also know of people who realised in their late thirties that they had pursued professions they were told to follow. I have a friend, a doctor by profession, who tried being the CEO of a hospital, which was doing well. He was doing well. But probably, there was some internal calling. In his early forties, he simultaneously started a café, and yes, you guessed it right—he is doing far better and is incredibly happy. I believe that a large portion of his happiness indeed comes from the loud fact that, despite being a fully qualified doctor, he followed his heart and made it.

There are no professional rules. Doctors change into medicolegal experts, lawyers change into life coaches. Anybody can change into an actor like how Boman Irani did. You can become a politician with an absolute age-no-bar clause in India.

We'll talk about strategies, sure. But more than that, we'll dive into why we owe it to ourselves to reconnect with what makes our hearts sing. It's about shifting gears from autopilot to 'heck yes, I'm doing this!' **It's about** being bold, a little reckless, and a lot honest with what we want the rest of our lives to look like.

Are you ready? Let's not settle for a quiet glide through midlife when we could be soaring. Join me, won't you, in turning the 'what-ifs' into 'why nots' and the 'someday' into 'today'. Because, my dear reader, if we're stirring up the pot anyway, we might as well make it interesting. Let's not just wake up to a new day but to a new way of seeing our lives full of potential, laughter, and yes, maybe a few good-natured eye rolls at how long we've waited.

THE POWER OF DREAMING BOLDLY

In the hustle of daily life, filled with its trials and tribulations, we often forget to pause and reflect on our dreams that truly keep us going. Have you ever considered the immense power that lies in dreaming? Whether it's a quiet wish whispered at night or a grand vision we declare loudly, dreams are the scaffolding of our personal growth and fulfilment.

In my career, where the days are often punctuated by difficult conversations, the importance of maintaining hope has never been clearer. Sharing tough news never gets easier, but it has deepened my conviction that we must never strip anyone of their hope. Hope and dreams steer us through stormy seas towards brighter horizons. Each day brings a new opportunity to dream, so why not grab that chance?

My elder brother often humorously quipped that **dreaming is the only thing that's still free (no taxes on dreams yet).** Isn't that a relief? Think about it: with thousands of thoughts crossing our minds each day, isn't it fascinating that the recurring ones often involve our deepest desires and dreams? If a dream keeps knocking on the door of your consciousness, maybe it's time to invite it in for tea and see what it wants to tell you.

Remember, the wildest dreams of yesterday are the reality of today. Did the dreamers of human flight or moon landings know their wild fantasies would one day be concrete achievements? Not at all! But they dared to dream big and take those initial, often shaky steps towards their goals. And that's exactly what I urge you to do. Dream big, ridiculously big! **Even if you don't catch the moon, you'll land among the stars, and along the way, you might just find that life becomes richer and more interesting.**

Once you start chasing your dreams, things begin to snowball: as you progress, opportunities multiply, and like-minded souls wander into your life.

As we wonder how we can turn these dreams from wisps of imagination into tangible realities, let's find inspiration from the stories of women, just like you and me, who decided that their middle years weren't the end of their story but a new, exhilarating beginning.

Ever toyed with the idea of turning a beloved hobby into a thriving business? Well, let me introduce you to Kalpana Jha and Uma Jha, two dynamic sisters-in-law from Bihar, who did just that with their venture, Jha Ji Store. After Kalpana's husband retired, they returned to their hometown of Darbhanga and went on an entrepreneurial journey with something as simple yet profound as traditional pickles, a beloved staple in every Indian household.

Now, their story isn't just about pickles; it's a narrative of dreams rejuvenated and realised. At an age when many might consider settling into the quiet rhythm of routine, these women decided to stir things up, quite literally, in their kitchen, with recipes handed down through generations. They started modestly, but their passion quickly scaled up, eventually landing them on India's popular TV show, "Shark Tank". While securing investment was a milestone, the real win was the affirmation of their dreams and capabilities.

This story is a striking reminder that it's never too late to start anew. Look around you, or better yet, look within. What's your "pickle recipe"? What's that passion brewing inside you, waiting to be shared with the world? Kalpana and Uma's journey from kitchen to boardroom illustrates beautifully that your age, background, or previous career choices don't cage your potential; they merely lay the groundwork for what's yet to come.

IDENTIFYING YOUR FORGOTTEN DREAMS

Have you ever wondered where dreams go when they're put on hold? Do they float around in limbo, waiting patiently for us to pick them back up, or do they silently fade away, buried under the layers of 'daily must-dos'? Well, it's time to bring them back into the light!

Now, how do we begin unravelling our tightly knit busy lives to find the threads of forgotten dreams? It starts with a bit of introspection. You might be thinking, "But I'm not much of a meditator!" Don't worry; you don't need to sit in silence for hours with incense burning in the background (unless, of course, you like ritualistic meditation) Let's try something a bit more active.

First, grab a journal or just a plain old piece of paper or whatever you have handy.

- What did I love to do as a child?

- What activities made me lose track of time?

- What were my biggest dreams and ambitions during my teenage years?

- What hobbies or activities brought me the most joy when I was young?

- Who were my role models, and what qualities did I admire in them?

- What subjects or topics fascinated me the most in school?

- How did I dream of my future when I was a teenager?

- What kind of impact did I dream of making on the world?

- What were the small, everyday things that excited me as a child?

- What talents or skills did I naturally excel at during my younger years?

- What were the dreams I shared with my friends and family?

These whimsical questions are the little keys that unlock the doors to our past passions.

Now, let's dig a bit deeper. Think about the last time you felt truly alive and excited. What were you doing? Maybe you were helping a friend decorate their home, and it sparked a forgotten passion for interior design, or perhaps you were organising a community event that reminded you how much you love bringing people together. Write down every single detail.

Sure, here are just the questions:

- What dreams have I been neglecting?

- Am I happy with my life now?

- Am I satisfied with my career?

- How can I reclaim my old dreams?

- What am I waiting for?

- What passions or interests did I have that I've set aside?

- What steps can I take today to move closer to my dreams?

- What fears or doubts are holding me back from pursuing my dreams?

- How can I overcome the obstacles that stand in my way?

- What small actions can I take each day to rekindle my passions?

- How can I incorporate my dreams into my current lifestyle?

- What would my younger self be proud of in my life today?

- Who can I reach out to for guidance or mentorship in reclaiming my dreams?

- How can I stay motivated and focused on my goals?

- What does success look like for me now, and how has it changed from my past vision?

You're standing at a crossroads, and the path you choose from here is entirely up to you.

Reflecting on these moments is an excavation of the self you've perhaps forgotten in the hustle and bustle of what we call 'adulting'. As you jot down these memories, you might feel a mix of nostalgia and excitement. It will be like finding an old photograph that reminds you of who you were before the world told you who you should be.

If you're feeling adventurous, turn this reflection into a guided meditation. Picture yourself in a cosy room filled with doors. Each door represents a path you might have taken, a dream you once had.

- Visualise the room. Imagine a room with countless doors, each one leading to a different dream you once held dear.

- As you open each door, allow yourself to fully visualise living out that dream. What does it look like? How does it feel?

- Engage your senses. What do you see, hear, smell, and touch in this dream world? Immerse yourself completely.

- Pay attention to how you feel as you explore these dreams. Are you excited, peaceful, nostalgic?

- Which dreams still resonate deeply with you? These are not just memories but potential aspirations for the future.

- Ask yourself which of these dreams could still be viable. Could they fit into your current life?

- Visualise how you could weave these dreams into your present reality. What steps would you need to take?

- Think about small, actionable steps you can take today to start reclaiming these dreams.

- Remember to stay positive and open-minded. Sometimes, the path to our dreams is winding and unexpected.

As you engage in this reflective exercise, you might discover dreams that still resonate deeply with you. Dreams become viable aspirations for the future. It's these discoveries that pave the way to the next step: reclaiming these dreams and weaving them into your current life.

It's never too late to reclaim old dreams, to rediscover paths not taken. I know people who changed tracks mid-journey to follow their true passions, proving it's possible to start anew, no matter where you are in life.

Commander R.S. Rathore, an Ex Naval officer in my extended family is an inspiring example. After years of dedicated service in the Indian Navy, he, felt a compelling urge to shift his course. Heeding his internal call, he retired early and founded his own academy, this time focusing on training Service Selection Board (SSB) aspirants. But he didn't stop there; he also authored *The Best Book for SSB, which is* now in its fifth edition, which has helped countless young people achieve their dreams of serving in the defence. In Commander Rathore's story, we see that success isn't just about following a set path—it's about paving a new one when your heart leads you elsewhere.

His story is a powerful reminder, that it's never too late to listen to your inner voice and reshape your destiny. Whether it's reviving an old dream or discovering a newfound calling, the second acts in our lives can be just as fulfilling, if not more, than the first. These journeys not only redefine success but also enrich the lives of those brave enough to take the leap.

STRATEGIES TO RECLAIM YOUR DREAMS

Rolling out the map for your dreams isn't quite like planning a vacation, but imagine if it were! You'd want to know exactly where you're going, what you'll do once you get there, and maybe where you'll have the best ice cream. Let's chart out our path to reclaim those dreams with a dash of spunk and a lot of determination.

Decode Your Dreams – First up, what exactly are your dreams? If they're a bit blurry, let's bring them into focus, like finding your spectacles first thing in the morning. Ah, there's the world! If they've been on the back burner for a while, they might be a little hazy. Pull out those notes from our earlier session. What caught your fire? Was it opening a boutique, writing poetry, penning a novel, turning your gardening hobby into a business or perhaps turning your grandmother's recipes into a cookbook? Detail these dreams out. Maybe create a vision board or keep a dream diary. Make a vision board or jot them down in a journal. Seeing your dreams in colour and on paper makes them less daunting and more doable, doesn't it?

Clear Your Doubts – Now, let's tackle those nagging doubts. Are your dreams just castles in the air? Remember, every castle starts with a foundation, even if it's built cloud-high! While it's normal to second-guess (after all, we're stepping into new territories), try to shake off the scepticism. How? By separating fear from prudence. Sift through those doubts and find out which ones are just old fears in disguise. Use your inner wisdom to tell the difference. Remember, for every person who says you can't, there's a part of you that knows you can. So, tune into that channel!

Overcome the Jitters – It's normal to feel jittery when embracing change and taking bold steps. Remember, the thrill of a roller coaster comes from its twists and turns. Life isn't much different. If you feel overwhelmed, take a deep breath and remember why you started. Connect with your support network, those cheerleaders who believe in your dreams even on days when you might doubt them.

Tackle Your fear of Failures – And then there's the fear of failure. Let's settle this once and for all—everyone fails. Yes, even that perfectly poised neighbour who seems to have her life together. Failure is not a sign to stop; it's merely a little bump in the road, a nudge to find a better path. Embrace failure as a mentor, not a tormentor. It teaches, guides, and, yes, sometimes pushes us in the mud, but hey, what's a little mud on your boots if you're on the road to success?

Makeover Your Mindset – It's easy to stick with the old script that says, "It's too late" or "That's not done." Well, guess what? Those scripts are overdue for a rewrite. Old conventions? Toss them out like last year's fashion faux pas. Just as sarees don't go out of style but get reinvented, so can your dreams. If someone tells you, "People your age don't start businesses," give them a cheeky grin and reply, "Maybe they just haven't met someone like me yet." Rewrite your script with beliefs that empower you, not tie you down. It's about breaking free from those limiting beliefs and showing what's possible when you dare to defy the norms.

Find Your Support System – Next, let's find your crowd. Navigating naysayers is one thing, but you need your own cheering squad. Connect with others who share your newfound passions. Find mentors who have danced this dance before, and join groups where sparks fly and ideas flourish. This is your tribe, the ones who cheer for you, offer a shoulder, and sometimes, a brilliant idea over a cup of chai. Dreams thrive in company, after all.

Make A Dream Blueprint – A dream without a plan is just a wish, isn't it? So, let's plot your path. What are your milestones? What practical steps do you need to take to bring this dream to life? Break them down. Need to learn a new skill? Find out where and how. Saving up for that dream project? Plan your finances. Turn your journey into a checklist and start ticking. Every small achievement is a step closer to your dream. Even the longest journey begins with a single step, or in our case, a single checklist!

Reignite Your Spark – If routine has dulled your sparkle, it's time to polish it up. It's time to reignite that inner spark. Shake up your routine, challenge yourself with something new every month, or dive headlong into projects that scare you just a bit. Ever thought of learning pottery? Or maybe taking up dancing? New experiences not only add spice to life but also recharge your batteries and keep you fired up about life. And trust me, enthusiasm is contagious and soon, you'll be drawing dreams and dreamers to you like a magnet! Who knows? It might spark up your next big idea.

Take the Leap – Now, how about we take some real steps? If your dream is to learn painting, sign up for that art class you've been eyeing. Or maybe you want to start a café? Start small. Organise a weekend pop-up café at a local fair. Dreaming of exploring new lands? Begin planning that trip, even if it's just a short excursion to a nearby town you've never visited. Each action, no matter how small, is a move towards your dream.

You can try practical, doable steps like:

- Read books, take online courses, and watch tutorials related to your goal.
- Break your dream into smaller, manageable goals to make it less overwhelming.

- Set a timeline for your goals to keep on track and motivated.

- Create a budget and outline your expenses to figure out how to fund your dream.

- Invest in the necessary tools and resources for your dream, like art supplies, kitchen equipment, or travel gear.

- Sign up for a class that aligns with your goal.

- Seek support from mentors for advice and encouragement.

- Join communities or groups related to your dream for support, ideas, and opportunities.

- Set up a dedicated space at home for your dream activities, such as a home studio or a desk for writing.

- Attend workshops, seminars, and events related to your dream for hands-on experience and networking.

- Use social media to share your journey and connect with a broader audience for feedback and accountability.

- Collaborate with others who share your passion to bring new perspectives and energy to your dream.

- Regularly track your progress with journals, apps, or spreadsheets to stay on course.

- Create a vision board with images, quotes, and goals that inspire you and keep your dream front and centre.

CONCLUSION:

As we wrap up this chapter, let's remember that change doesn't require a grand, sweeping leap into the unknown. Think of it more like a delightful series of hops, skips, and jumps towards the life you envision for yourself.

Don't wait for a perfect day, another 'perfect' moment, or another sign from the universe. The perfect time to act is now. Set a simple, achievable goal for today. It could be something as delightful as wearing that bold red lipstick to the office or as bold as signing up for that painting class you've always thought about. And as you march towards your dreams, remember to tread gently, ensuring your pursuits harm no one. This is your life, your masterpiece to create; paint it with bold strokes and bright colours, but always with respect and consideration for others around you. So, what will your first step be?

Reclaiming your dreams means finding the courage to pursue what sets your soul on fire, regardless of the obstacles that stand in your way.

Chapter 4

PRINCIPLE 2: COMMAND YOUR COURSE – EMBRACE SELF-LEADERSHIP

"Mastering others is strength; mastering oneself is true power."

— Lao Tsu.

Have you ever found yourself daydreaming at an airport, lost between the pages of a book while waiting for a flight? That was me in the summer when my daughter was gearing up to fly the nest for college. We were at Indira Gandhi International Airport Terminal 2, waiting for our flight from Bhopal to Srinagar via Delhi, heading for a much-needed holiday in Kashmir. I wandered into a bookstore and picked up *Maybe You Should Talk to Someone* by Lori Gottlieb. One chapter, humorously titled "Only if the Queen Had Balls," struck a chord with me, resonating deeply. It reflected a sentiment many of us know all too well – "I wanted to do so much, but my family didn't allow me, my in-laws didn't, my circumstances didn't." Sounds familiar, doesn't it?

Stop for a moment and ask yourself (be brutally honest because this is a private chat with your deepest self): did they really stop you, or was it easier to go with the flow? Did you choose the path of least resistance? If it's the former, now, in midlife, it might be your chance to appeal that old decision. After years of investment and proof of your capabilities, isn't it fair to claim a little something for yourself? With the kids more independent and your spouse a bit more mature (hopefully), isn't it time to ask for your turn?

Life, especially in middle age, can often feel like something that just happens to us. But what if you could take control? Imagine swapping that passenger seat for the driver's. What if, instead of being tossed about by life's currents, you could steer your own course? This isn't about being pushed by the winds of circumstance but about being the wind itself.

This chapter is all about changing how you view your role in your own life. It's about moving from just going with the flow to taking charge of your own destiny. It's not only about dealing with what life throws at you but reshuffling the cards and creating a new hand that gets you pumped. So, as we dive into the journey of self-leadership, let's chat about how you can fully embrace this role. How can you switch from being passive to being more hands-on? Are you game to take the lead? Because, my dear reader, this is where your real adventure kicks off.

Let's start with the small, everyday choices. Breaking the patterns others expect us to follow isn't just about big declarations; it's about the little moments, the daily decisions that say, "This is my life, and I decide how to live it." **Remember, allowing others to walk over you doesn't earn respect; it only invites disrespect.** It's time to assert that you will not accept poor treatment, not from strangers and certainly not from those closest to you.

People may not always realise how their actions affect us. A lack of emotional intelligence can blind them to the impact they have. But remember, you are in control of your narrative. Playing the victim won't change your situation; taking charge of your life will. Your life is your canvas. No one else knows the dreams of your youth or has the right to dictate your future. So, take charge now, for your fulfilment and peace.

I know someone, a dedicated school teacher, who was entangled in a marriage that had grown toxic over the years. With a daughter nearing college age, this woman made a life-altering decision. As her daughter prepared to step into her own future, the lady filed for divorce, choosing to not only leave her strained relationship behind but to also seek a new beginning.

Together with her daughter, she moved to Delhi, where her unwavering dedication and extensive teaching experience won her the role of vice-principal at a prestigious school. Her journey didn't stop there. Driven by a relentless conviction to push beyond the ordinary and refuse to settle, she climbed the ranks to become the principal. Today, she is not just leading her school but also serving as a senior coordinator for the Central Board of Secondary Education (CBSE).

Her success extends beyond academic administration. She has become a familiar face on television, discussing educational strategies and school leadership, demonstrating the influence and respect she commands in her field. She celebrates her freedom and new life by travelling the world with her daughter. This woman's story is proof of the power of determination and the courage to reclaim one's life.

RECOGNISING PASSIVITY

Continuing our chat about pushing against the tides of passivity, let's consider that there's absolutely no harm in pushing a little harder, especially now. If you think about it, you've got the time. Maybe not unlimited time, but certainly enough to make a splash. I keep emphasising this because it's so crucial. Yes, when you start changing things, you'll likely meet resistance. It's natural. People around you, just like you, are snug in their comfort zones, the ones you've helped maintain. And who can blame them?

But here's where you need to be a tad strategic. Work out a reasonable plan, be justified, rational, then lay your proposal out there. Remember, though, while you may need the support of those around you, you should never seek approval for your dreams. Maybe that's where things got sticky before, right? Seeking nods for your dreams instead of channelling your energy into figuring out how to realise them.

If you find yourself acknowledging that nobody really stopped you from pursuing your dreams, that perhaps it was a bit of laziness or lack of that initial effort, it's time for a gentle shake-up. Start working out the logistics. Because deep down, if there was ever something you wanted to do, something you were capable of, and the only thing missing was your action. It's going to sting someday if you don't address it.

Let me share a bit of my story. Being the youngest of three siblings, I was always the talkative one. I still am. I love to talk. It's part of who I am. As I grew older, especially out of school and away from home, I realised that being chatty wasn't always appreciated, especially by those in positions of power. Perhaps because it made me popular, accepted, and, yes, even admired. And what do all the grown-up, adult, mature preachings tell us? "Listen more, talk less." And so, I learned to become a careful speaker.

But here's the twist … all those conversations that used to buzz around in my head, all those pent-up words, have found their way onto the paper you're reading now. Here I am, living my dream of writing a book. Today is the day I have always imagined. Guess what? In fulfilling my dream, I'm not harming anyone or sacrificing any of my roles, be it as a medical teacher, a practising gynaecologist, a mother, a wife, or a friend. Each role that I embody remains intact.

So, as we move forward, let's keep in mind that changing your course doesn't mean neglecting your duties or stepping on toes. It's about adding another dimension to who you are. And who says you can't add colourful layers to your life's canvas? Let's start painting with bold, broad strokes, shall we? Let's not wait for another day, another perfect moment, or another sign. The perfect time is now.

MINDSET SHIFT

Have you ever caught yourself thinking, "I just can't catch a break!" or maybe, "Why does this always happen to me?". It's easy to feel like the universe is conspiring against us. But let's take a moment here. What we're diving into today is about changing that narrative from feeling like life's perpetual victim to seeing yourself as the bold author of your own story.

You know, many of us believe that when someone hinders another's growth, they must be acutely aware of their actions. I often hear friends debate heatedly – how can people be at peace with themselves after deliberately stunting someone else's development? Here's a thought – often, wrongdoers either lack the insight to recognise the damage they're causing or are cruel and selfish enough to purposefully do so. They might even believe you deserve such treatment or think they are entitled to act this way without any concern for overstepping boundaries at your expense.

So, what's our move in such scenarios? Should we sit back quietly, waiting for them to realise their mistakes? That would hardly be effective. Instead, it's crucial to stand up, be honest, and communicate. Bottling up emotions is harmful, not just to individuals but to families and organisations, too. It's important to express your feelings and communicate clearly that if people in any relationship or situation aren't growing together, they're inevitably going to grow apart. Growth is an inescapable law of life. Things, situations, people, and relationships cannot remain static. **Change is the only constant, but we can direct some of that change**.

Shifting into a mindset of empowerment begins with rejecting the victim script. It requires believing that you are capable and deserving of steering your own ship. Think of yourself as the captain, not just a passenger along for the ride. How do we get there? By flipping the script that whispers we're lacking or need a saviour, let's pen a new narrative: "I'm plenty and the author of my tale." Transform from damsel to hero, or better yet, the wise wizard shaping destiny. Grab the reins or the wand, and enchant the life you desire.

As Farah Gray put it, **"Build your dreams, or someone will hire you to build theirs."** This isn't just a call to action, but it's a necessity. Taking control of your dreams and aspirations is all about deciding the path your life takes.

Changing your mindset kicks off with a simple yet deep realisation – you deserve to lead your own life. It's not about being selfish; it's about understanding that you can't give if you're running on empty. How can you support others if you haven't cared for yourself first?

Let's try something. Remember a moment when you felt super confident. It may be when you nailed a project at work, solved a tough problem at home, or just got something small done that made you proud. Hold on to that feeling. That's the real you. That's the you who doesn't just go with the flow but actively shapes it.

Now, imagine tackling each day with that swagger. Envision yourself not deciding out of fear or duty but from a place of strength and belief in your skills. It might seem a tad odd at first, like test-driving a new outfit that isn't quite "you" yet. But trust me, it's a looker, and the more you rock it, the more it'll click.

Ever catch those scenes in movies where someone unexpectedly steps up as the boss? Cue the montage of them slaying tasks, making boss moves, and looking undeniably slick! Why not picture your life with its own montage? You, making bold decisions, you, stepping up in meetings, you, turning your passions into projects. Why shouldn't your life have those highlight reels?

Remember, viewing yourself as capable and deserving isn't about having all the answers or never facing doubt. It's all about trusting that you've got what it takes to find the answers, learn from the challenges and lead. It's about changing that voice inside your head that tells you you're not good enough.

BUILDING SELF-RELIANCE

Building self-reliance is essentially about making decisions that reflect your true self. Let's dive deeper into this transformative process, ensuring each step is taken with confidence and a sprinkle of humour, as we usually do!

Decision-making can be nerve-wracking, right? You're not alone if the thought of making a big decision sends you into a spin. Sometimes, just the swirl of details can cloud your judgment. Here's a nifty trick to clear that fog – imagine a friend comes to you with the exact same decision to make. What advice would you give them? Surprisingly, when we think about helping someone else, our thoughts tend to become clearer and more rational. Apply this "outsider" perspective to your own decisions. It's like taking a step back for a clearer view. However, never forget that it's great to hear others' opinions, but the final call is yours. Why? Because no one knows your life as intimately as you do. Everyone sees the world through their own lens, shaped by personal fears, strengths, and experiences. Your friends and family know you well, but they don't feel your feelings or think your thoughts. Their advice, though well-meaning, is coloured by their perceptions and life experiences. **At the end of the day, there cannot be a better best friend to you than yourself.**

Being real with yourself is key. Often, we dodge decisions out of fear of messing up. That fear can push us to sit back and let others call the shots. But when you surrender that choice, you hand over the reins of your life. And if things go south, blaming them is easy, but it's not the answer. Blame stalls us; action drives us onward.

So, if you find yourself hesitating to make a decision, take a moment to reflect. Are you avoiding a decision because you're truly unsure, or are you afraid of taking responsibility for the outcome? Being honest about this can be a game-changer. It shifts your mindset from avoidance to ownership.

Taking charge of your decisions is empowering. It's like you're creating your own story, not just going with the flow of life. Your life is a bunch of stories, and guess what? You're the main character. So, why would you let someone else hold the pen?

Consider each decision as a pivotal moment in your story. With each choice, you're writing the next chapter. Sure, not every decision will be perfect. Some will lead to great outcomes, others might teach you hard lessons. But each one is a step forward in your journey of self-discovery and self-reliance.

Let's also remember that being decisive doesn't mean you're inflexible. It means you're committed to living intentionally, making choices that align with who you are and who you want to be. And yes, part of living intentionally is being prepared to pivot when necessary. Life is unpredictable, and our ability to adapt is just as important as our ability to plan.

Incorporate a daily practice of decision-making in your routine. Start with something small each day. Choose a new route to work, try a new recipe, or decide to start a book you've been curious about. Each small decision builds your confidence and hones your ability to make bigger, more significant choices down the road.

Also, sprinkle some lightness into your decision-making process. It doesn't have to be all serious business! Treat it like a game. Try different moves, take notes, and hey, it's okay to chuckle at blunders. After all, the world won't implode over a tiny misstep. What truly matters is your growth and fine-tuning what clicks for you.

When we had shifted into a new house in a new locality, we started visiting a nearby supermarket for our regular grocery shopping. In fact, with my kids being toddlers, it used to be quite an event for them, running around the not-so-big departmental store, sometimes messing up the racks and once even smashing a glass ketchup bottle by dropping it straight down simply because I shouted from a distance, "Don't pick that up."

Anyhow, incidents like these gave me the opportunity to connect with the most humble, traditional North Indian Marwari lady at the cash counter, who appeared intelligent and educated. My gynaecologist profile sometimes allows me to connect with women quite easily, so I learned that she was actually a finance graduate in her mid-forties. She got married just after graduation into a Marwari joint family, where working for women would go against the family's reputation, so she started living a traditional Indian homemaker's life.

Their joint family broke apart after her father-in-law's untimely death and poor distribution of financial rights, and so did the family business. Her husband, unable to carry forward their dry fruit business, started finding it difficult to sustain the family's demands. He was a twelfth-pass, and his male ego did not allow him to accept his wife's help either. He started avoiding the family and spending more time outside the home. Helpless as to how to raise the kids, this lady took a little financial help from her father and started taking online home delivery orders for groceries, running it from her house (those were not the days of Blinkit or BigBasket).

Gradually, as this venture started generating revenue, she gained some confidence from her husband, who was practically broke by then, and renovated their house to convert the ground floor into a departmental store. As her kids were also growing up, practically working from home worked well for her. I remember that this store used to close between 2–4 pm for a lunch break in those times, and I understand why. And there she was, the saviour who sailed her family out of all the mess and, yes, restored that Dhanna Seth status of her husband as well, quietly sitting at the cash counter, with all that confidence in her skin, with the expression, "No issues, you be the boss," very well knowing who she is, what she is capable of, with no need to be loud or prove herself.

That is what I talk about in this book. It is not always necessary to be in a rebel mode, taking up confrontations and declaring battles. No, please, they are a waste of time and energy, and no one deserves that level of your strength wasted. But **what is absolutely essential is knowing your goal, being confident, totally trusting yourself, being consistent (half-hearted attempts fail), and hitting hard with conviction.** If you are able to keep everyone together, you will have people to celebrate your success. If you lose all of them, half of them will still come back; that's the rule. If you lose some, you won't regret much because, in the journey, you will find yourself, and that's someone worth finding.

FROM PASSIVE TO PROACTIVE

Switching from a passive style to a more hands-on approach in life isn't just limited to decision-making. It's about being a go-getter, an instigator, someone who takes charge with confidence. Ready to turn those "someday" dreams into "today" actions?

- **Start off with Small, Purposeful Steps**

    Begin by identifying some simple, achievable steps that can kickstart significant changes. Want to improve your health? Swap evening snacks for a short stroll in your neighbourhood or the park. Interested in taking up a new hobby or skill? Allocate about 30 minutes daily (maybe during your commute or instead of watching TV) to explore something new, like a language app or free online courses.

- **Set Daily Intentions**

Each morning, take a moment to write down what you want to achieve for the day. Use a small diary or an app on your phone to keep track. It could be as simple as finishing a report for work, calling an old friend, or preparing a healthy meal for dinner. This daily habit not only sets the tone for a productive day but also helps instil a sense of purpose and direction.

- **Weekly Check-In:**

Take a moment each week to reflect on your progress. Whether it's Sunday afternoon or another quiet time, think about your wins and areas for growth. It's not about being self-critical or hard on yourself, but about building self-awareness and gearing up for the week ahead.

- **Embrace Flexibility in Your Goals**

Life's full of surprises, especially in bustling cities like India's, where a sudden bandh or family duty can derail your plans. Adapt your goals as required. If you miss a target, tweak it instead of giving up. Being flexible can keep you motivated and ease the stress of high expectations.

- **Celebrate Your Progress**

Recognise and reward yourself for the progress you make, no matter how small. Completed a week of yoga classes? Treat yourself to a movie or a small outing to your favourite chaat spot. These little celebrations provide positive reinforcement, making your proactive journey enjoyable and sustainable.

- **Seek Feedback and Support**

  Build a support network of friends, family, or colleagues who encourage your proactive lifestyle. Share your goals with them and ask for feedback. This can be particularly helpful in a culture where community and familial bonds play a crucial role in personal success. Plus, having someone to share your journey with can make the process less daunting and more fun.

CONCLUSION:

As we wrap up our journey through transforming from passive to proactive, let's remember a vital truth. Those around us, like our spouses, children, bosses, colleagues and friends, while often well-intentioned and truly caring, are navigating their own paths as well. They make decisions that seem right for us, but these decisions are naturally influenced by their perspectives and needs, not just ours. Isn't it interesting how even the most caring folks tend to prioritise their own needs, sometimes without even realising it? So, what does this mean for you? It means that while it's perfectly fine to appreciate and trust the advice of others, you also have the ability and the right to make your own decisions. This isn't about disregarding their input but about stepping into your role as the architect of your destiny. You have the power to navigate your own path, to make decisions that resonate with your core values and aspirations. You're not just playing a part in someone else's story; you're the director of your own life narrative.

It's never too late. When you start making decisions, you might worry about making mistakes. After all, everyone, even the best, can slip up. But don't let fear of error stop you. Decisions are made with the best intentions and the information available at the time. They are the right choices for that moment. Only hindsight might show us otherwise.

Embrace the understanding that every decision has its flip side; nothing is purely black or white. By actively making choices and taking responsibility for those choices, you shape your life precisely how you envision it. This proactive stance ensures that you have fewer regrets when you look back at your life. Each decision, each action, is a brushstroke in the masterpiece that is your life.

And remember, steering your own course doesn't have to be a grave or solemn task. Treat it like an adventure. Laugh at your mistakes, learn from them, and keep going. Celebrate your victories, no matter how small. Every step forward is a step in the right direction.

So, as we conclude this chapter, ask yourself – Are you ready to be the decision-maker in your own life? Are you prepared to craft a future that resonates with who you are and who you want to be? After all, this is your life, your story. How will you choose to write the next chapter?

Chapter 5

PRINCIPLE 3: REDEFINE CONNECTIONS – REVITALISE RELATIONSHIPS

"Evaluating the benefits and drawbacks of any relationship is your responsibility. You do not have to passively accept what is brought to you. You can choose."

— Deborah Ray

Welcome to a crucial chapter in our journey together. Have you ever thought about how the people in our lives influence who we are and who we become? It's like being part of a garden where each relationship is a different plant; some are blooming beautifully, encouraging us to grow, while others might need a bit of pruning to bring out their best and our best.

So, why is it essential to ensure that our relationships support our personal growth? Imagine trying to thrive in a space where you're constantly overshadowed. Not so easy, right? Just as a plant struggles to grow in the shade, we, too, can find ourselves wilting if our connections don't provide the right environment of support and sunlight. Along with gelling well or having fun together, it should be about nurturing relationships that truly enrich us, that make us more of who we are, not less.

Think about the last time you felt truly supported in a decision that was crucial for your personal development. Felt good, didn't it? Now, consider the opposite. Think about those times when you felt held back or misunderstood by those closest to you. Quite stifling, isn't it? This chapter isn't about assigning blame but about taking a proactive look at our relationships and deciding which ones we need to nurture, adjust, or, sometimes, let go.

In India, where relationships are deeply woven into the fabric of our lives, redefining them is not only personal, but also revolutionary. Here, family and community ties are strong, but this strength need not be a barrier to personal growth. Instead, it can be the very foundation on which we build a network of support and encouragement.

As we delve into this topic, I want you to remember: **the goal isn't to cut ties or create distance. Instead, it's about reshaping these connections to be more mutually empowering.** Are you ready to take a closer look at your relationships? Are you prepared to make the adjustments necessary to ensure they not only survive but thrive, thereby supporting your journey towards becoming the best version of yourself?

ASSESSING CURRENT RELATIONSHIPS

As we move through this part, imagine it like having a heart-to-heart with an old pal – that's me! We're going to discuss some tough questions that could steer your journey in a positive direction.

So, let's kick things off with a straightforward yet impactful question – **Are your relationships lifting you up or weighing you down?**

Imagine each relationship as a balloon. Some balloons help you soar, reaching new heights, filled with encouragement and joy. Others weigh you down like they're filled with lead, dragging you while you're trying to rise. Reflect on which relationships leave you feeling invigorated and which ones leave you feeling exhausted. Good relationships will be fun and will make you feel supported, inspired, and valued.

Now, let's chat about boundaries, those invisible lines that show how much we let others sway our lives. Do the people near you really get these lines? Like a buddy who rings you up late at night when you're chilling or a family member who assumes you'll always be there for them. In good relationships, they value your time, your personal space, and your vibes. They don't nudge you out of your comfort zone without checking in with you first.

Next, let's address a tougher subject – Are any of your relationships holding you back from chasing your dreams? Sometimes, without even realising it, we might be tethered to someone who doesn't want us to change. **They might fear that your growth could mean less time or affection for them.**

It's essential to recognise these dynamics because reclaiming your dreams might require some space from these relationships. Remember that the people we surround ourselves with have an immense impact on our mindset, motivation, and overall ability to pursue our dreams. By taking an honest look at your current relationships, you start to see which ones truly empower you and which might be creating barriers.

However, when you look at your relationships, it's not about pointing fingers or starting drama. It's about making sure your inner circle – the people you share your life with – are on the same page and cheering you on as you grow. This could mean having some tough talks, setting clearer boundaries, or maybe deciding to distance yourself from relationships that aren't helping you. So, ask yourself – which relationships bring you joy, and which could use a little rethinking? Don't be afraid to make changes that put your well-being first. Your relationships should lift you up, not bring you down.

Ready to make some adjustments? Let's do this with kindness and courage, making sure our connections are healthy and uplifting. Because, hey, in the end, it's not just about being connected but also being enriched by those connections.

SETTING HEALTHY BOUNDARIES AND RESHAPING DYNAMICS

Growing up involves a continuous process of discovering ourselves and our surroundings, which includes the people around us and various situations we encounter. Often, many of us fear upsetting others or saying no. Have you ever wondered why this is? It largely stems from a human desire for acknowledgement and acceptance. We fear rejection and abandonment. This fear can be especially pronounced in women, who are typically more tolerant, adaptive, and resilient by nature. This doesn't mean that women don't have their own desires or goals; however, they often put these aside for the sake of larger family needs or simply to avoid confrontations, thereby forgetting to prioritise themselves.

One of my friends struggled every single day because of the lack of support and consideration from her husband. During the busiest times of their lives, when family commitments were at its peak, she found herself running the household without much support. She had to handle most of the demands of raising kids, ensuring the house was in order, meeting professional commitments and deadlines, and finding new opportunities. Whenever she had a deadline to meet that would require her to work till late at night, she would have to pack up the household and put the kids to sleep before working against the clock. Mind you, she would also have to wake up early and get things running with barely any sleep after all this.

Especially during complicated times like these, when she was emotionally and physically drained, her husband would initiate intimacy, justifying it as the best method to relax. He didn't realise that his wife needed overall support, space and emotional intimacy. After years of tolerating this behaviour, one day she knew she couldn't continue like this anymore. She knew it was time for a change and took the initiative to confront her husband and express clearly that she wanted things to change for the relationship to continue. It took time, but her husband came around and started being more empathetic, understanding and supportive.

My friend believes that it's the inner strength she felt on that day that saved her marriage. It helped her speak up and ask for what she needed. It helped her husband see the truth. She says that she's glad she tried to solve the issue before taking drastic measures like ending the relationship. **Sometimes, the simple act of speaking up can change one's life.**

In any relationship, it's rare for both parties to be on exactly the same page. Usually, one person is more invested, more in love, and more in need of the connection. To this person, the relationship holds more significance than it does to their partner, who may only care out of convenience, allowing the relationship to continue without much personal investment. The problem here is that the partner who is more invested often ends up hurt, crying more frequently, yet still desiring to maintain the status quo. Unfortunately, this isn't a fair deal. They may feel obliged by the other's allowance to stay in the relationship, taking on increasing responsibilities while their partner enjoys their freedom, until they are left completely drained and exhausted.

In an ideal world, such unequal relationships would be reevaluated and possibly ended. However, distancing oneself from a source of constant pain is not always feasible. But, what if you could attempt to shift the balance? What if, just for a trial, you stood up and told yourself that you don't need this relationship and its associated mess? Let things fall apart. To your surprise, you might find that this change prompts your partner to start rescuing the relationship, suddenly caring for you in ways they hadn't before.

Don't let anyone take advantage of your kindness or exploit you unilaterally because you fear the consequences, like children suffering, meals not being ready, or the house falling into disarray. As long as you remain protective of maintaining a perfect facade, there are chances that your partner will keep you under constant threat, manipulating you in their favour. For once, bring things to equal terms. If they don't love or care enough, reflect that. If they truly view you as a liability, then now is the time to take your stand and evaluate how much you really need them and whether you can refuse to tolerate toxicity in the relationship.

As we journey through the intricate paths of our relationships and personal growth, we're often met with a conundrum – how to balance the pursuit of our dreams with the steadfast commitments we've made along the way. It's vital to reflect on these commitments, not as burdens but as essential elements of our journey that mould who we are and who we aim to become.

Whether it's a marriage, parenthood, or a career, these commitments are choices you make intentionally. They aren't just responsibilities; they are pledges of integrity, parts of your identity that you've promised to nurture.

However, fulfilling these roles doesn't mean sidelining your own dreams. It's about finding a harmonious balance. Remember, escaping to the proverbial Himalayas might seem tempting when faced with tough choices, but real peace comes from confronting issues head-on, not avoiding them. It involves crafting solutions that align with your deepest values and needs, enhancing your life's quality without compromising your integrity.

But here's where the delicate balance comes into play – prioritising relationships over being right. It's tempting to want to win every argument, to stand firm on every issue, but consider the old wisdom that **winning an argument isn't worth losing a relationship**. True strength lies in knowing which battles to fight and which to let go, ensuring that the relationships that truly matter are nurtured, not neglected.

Sometimes, to maintain harmony, it might be necessary to let the other person "win." This doesn't mean losing control over your life; rather, it's about understanding that compromise can encourage a healthier, more supportive environment. Reflect on the importance of each relationship. Are they contributing to your growth, or are they relics of who you used to be? Prioritise those that encourage you to be your best self.

As you reassess these dynamics, remember to stay true to your essence. Every decision you make, be it personal or professional, should reflect your true desires and circumstances, not merely conform to external expectations. This authenticity is what sets the foundation for relationships that are not only enduring but also empowering.

Setting boundaries is also key. They aren't barriers but markers that define how others can interact with you respectfully. For instance, if you decide not to take work calls after a certain hour to spend time with your family or on a personal hobby, communicate this boundary clearly and consistently. This isn't about isolation but about ensuring that your relationships respect your space, allowing you to grow both personally and professionally.

Facing resistance is inevitable as you redefine these boundaries. People are comfortable with the status quo and may see your growth as a threat to their comfort. However, armed with honesty and a clear understanding of your needs, stand firm. Communicate effectively that growth is non-negotiable and changes in relationships are necessary for mutual benefit.

Lastly, integrate your roles seamlessly. Whether as a parent, spouse, or professional, ensure that each role you play supports and does not detract from your personal growth. Each decision, each action should be a step towards a life where you are not just fulfilling obligations but are actively pursuing a fulfilling, authentic existence.

By maintaining this balance, by reshaping relationships to support your journey, and by being true to your commitments and dreams, you craft a life not dictated by circumstances but designed by your deepest convictions and aspirations.

Sometimes, it's easy to get stuck in the web of our own expectations, especially when it comes to how we think others should understand us.

We often expect others to instinctively know what we need or want, expecting those around us to understand our desires without us having to express them. This leads to piling up small grievances that make everyday life more difficult. Consider the nights wasted feeling upset, waiting for a partner to offer comfort they don't realise you need, followed by days spoiled by disappointment and discomfort. But is it really fair to presume that anyone can fully understand what's going on inside us?

On a lighter note, are we even fully in tune with ourselves? Perhaps it's more reasonable for us to take responsibility for communicating our needs and expectations. If we find ourselves disappointed, maybe we should examine whether we've clearly expressed what we wanted or needed in the first place. After all, humans have the unique gift of verbal expression, a tool that isn't available to all creatures. Why not use it?

Often, you might find that you haven't voiced your needs because you're unclear in your own mind, afraid of rejection, or perhaps driven by an unnecessary sense of pride. These are personal challenges that need addressing on our end. Expressing yourself might sometimes lead to surprising revelations. Perhaps what you perceived as suffering due to others overstepping your boundaries was really just a simple misunderstanding—a problem because you didn't explicitly communicate your boundaries.

So, is it truly fair to feel victimised and blame others? More often than not, speaking up can clarify misunderstandings and relieve unnecessary emotional strain. So, is it really fair to feel victimised and blame others? Engaging in open communication can prevent a lot of this distress and foster better understanding and stronger relationships. Let's not underestimate the power of simply expressing what's on our minds.

NURTURING SUPPORTIVE CONNECTIONS

In the journey of nurturing supportive connections, a crucial yet often overlooked aspect is the prioritisation of one's own well-being. True relationship health flourishes not just through mutual support but also through individual strength and happiness.

When you prioritise your own well-being, you set a foundation for relationships that are not only supportive but also sustainable. Think of it this way – if you continuously deplete your reserves to satisfy others, what's left for you? This approach can lead to feelings of being overlooked and undervalued, causing strain and eventual deterioration in even the strongest bonds.

Why let it reach that breaking point? Recognising the importance of setting boundaries early is key to preventing others from overstepping, thus maintaining the health of your relationships. This concept became vividly clear to me through the example set by my mother-in-law, a distinguished Bengali gynaecologist, whose method of coping with marital tensions taught me invaluable lessons about personal space and self-care.

Despite her professional accolades and intellectual prowess, she, like many, navigated her share of family challenges. Her technique for managing stress and asserting her need for space was both subtle and powerful. In her living room stood a cushioned chair facing the television, a sanctuary where she would retreat with a stern expression and a poised demeanour whenever tensions arose. This chair was her fortress, an invisible circle around herself that none could penetrate except her beloved grandchildren. Observing her for over fifteen years, I learned the profound impact of such a personal sanctuary.

This story underscores a pivotal lesson – creating physical and emotional boundaries is crucial. It's not about isolation but about defining a space where you can recharge and reflect, free from external pressures. Implementing this in our lives means actively setting aside time and space that is ours alone, where our needs take precedence.

Moreover, prioritising well-being also involves making thoughtful decisions that reflect our personal values and desires. Each decision, from how we manage our time to the company we keep, shapes the quality of our lives. If we continuously compromise our well-being for the sake of others, we not only harm ourselves but also set a precedent that invites further encroachments into our personal boundaries.

In nurturing supportive connections, remember to cultivate relationships that respect and encourage these boundaries. Engage with people who understand the value of personal space and who support you in maintaining it. These connections should uplift you, bringing joy and energy rather than draining your resources.

Hey, why not have open chats about your needs and boundaries with your friends and family? Good communication clears things up, so they get your space and limits. Plus, it lets them share their boundaries too, building respect and stronger bonds.

In summary, as we continue to build and nurture supportive relationships, let us not forget the foundational role our well-being plays in this process. By prioritising our mental, emotional, and physical health, we enhance our capacity to support others and create deeper, more meaningful connections. Let this be a reminder to all of us to ensure that each relationship we cultivate is rooted in respect, support, and mutual growth.

CONCLUSION:

As we close this chapter on revitalising our relationships, let's reflect on the profound transformations we've undertaken. Redefining our connections isn't merely about managing our social circles; it's a deeper call to ensure that every relationship genuinely nurtures our growth and respects our boundaries.

However, it's crucial to balance this pursuit with your existing responsibilities. Maintaining your commitments is part of being a person of integrity. True peace comes from resolving issues, not avoiding them. It involves finding solutions that resonate with your personal values and needs.

But there's a delicate balance to maintain. In any relationship, finding a balance where both parties feel like winners is ideal but not always possible. If a relationship is important to you, sometimes letting the other person "win" can uphold a healthier, more supportive environment. This doesn't mean losing control over your life; rather, it's about choosing your battles wisely and focusing on maintaining harmony and showing care for those you value. That's what truly matters Your role within your family or any other important group should reflect your personal goals and values. Whether you see yourself as the nucleus of your family or as playing another central role, your actions should strive to maintain the integrity and happiness of that group. It's about proactive harmony and not just about individual wins. Crafting the life you want involves making thoughtful decisions that enhance the well-being of both you and your loved ones.

Moreover, always stay true to yourself in whatever decisions you make. Your actions should align with your own values and desires and not just be performed out of obligation or expectation.

I'm not suggesting that the life you've led so far was misguided. Rather, I'm urging you to pause and reflect on two crucial questions – Are you satisfied with your life as it's been, and do you want to continue in the same vein? With life's ever-changing variables like health, emotions, family, finances, and career, it's vital to reassess whether your current path will still suit your future needs.

Let this chapter be a reminder that you have the power to shape your relational world. As you turn each page and face each day, remember that every relationship offers an opportunity to reinforce your values and expand your horizons. Carry this knowledge into every interaction, and let it guide you to more fulfilling connections.

Here's to growing together with those around us and building relationships that are not only supportive but transformative. As you continue on your path, let the insights from this chapter inspire you to create a network of relationships that reflects the very best of who you are and all that you strive to become.

Chapter 6

PRINCIPLE 4: CAREER REBOOT – TRANSFORM YOUR CAREER

"The truth is that our finest moments are most likely to occur when we are feeling deeply uncomfortable, unhappy, or unfulfilled. For it is only in such moments, propelled by our discomfort, that we are likely to step out of our ruts and start searching for different ways or truer answers."

— M. Scott Peck

THE IMPORTANCE OF A CAREER

Our careers often hold a mirror to our deepest selves, revealing layers not just of our talents but also our dreams. A job isn't just a job… it is somehow a part of our identity. When we meet someone new, isn't one of the first questions we ask, "What do you do?" This question is a glimpse into what drives a person, what they're passionate about, what they're capable of. And how often do we introduce ourselves through our professions, only to realise that these roles define our societal image? Yet, beyond societal views, our careers should resonate with our inner spirits, should they not?

Now, think of the joy that pulses through you when you're engaged in work that feels meaningful. It's like finding a rare treasure in an unexpected place. When you have the kind of career that aligns with your inner values, it does more than just fill your pockets; it enriches your spirit and energises your days. However, embracing such fulfilment in work is often overshadowed by societal stereotypes, especially for women at the midlife juncture, a time when many assume it's too late to chase new dreams or shift careers. Yet, **how can it be too late when life still calls us to contribute, learn, and grow?**

Our careers should be a reflection of our aspirations, not a resignation to circumstances. If you feel stuck or unfulfiled, ask yourself whether your current path reflects your deepest desires or if it merely follows a script laid out by others' expectations. Breaking away from these moulds isn't just about personal happiness. It's a reclaiming of one's narrative, a declaration that even in midlife, the pen is in your hand, ready to script the next chapter. So, let's not dim the light that personal fulfilment brings.

I remember as kids, we would often complain that we couldn't handle geography or that history was not our cup of tea, etc. I had a paternal uncle who was a wing commander in the Indian Air Force, and he would always tell us that, for a scholar with brains, subjects are not limiting. A genuine scholar will handle maths as well as they handle psychology, at least until the school level. Toppers don't complain. They simply know the technique to master. Yes, we do see in each year's results, kids securing 100% in all subjects (though I accept individual talents do matter when it comes to specialising and mastering). So, never feel that if you are stuck in a certain profession, you need to die in the same field. If you feel you are good at something, please try doing it before letting it go. This same uncle eventually took early voluntary retirement from the Air Force and went on to become a writer, a social reformer, imparting education to poor kids and widowed or abandoned women.

STANDING UP FOR ONESELF IN ONE'S PROFESSION

When you are part of any organisation, standing firm on your professional ground is a right. Think of your workplace like a new relationship. From the get-go, it's vital to establish who you are, what you bring to the table, and, importantly, how you expect to be treated. To be frank, it's rarely about garnering attention for what you expect in return, but more about asserting how you allow others to interact with you. **Stopping them from treating you like a doormat is your responsibility, because if you allow one person to ill-treat you publicly, it's contagious. It sends a message to many more.**

Reflecting on a personal story from my early days post-college at a crowded maternity hospital, the environment was intense, to say the least. In such high-stakes settings, senior staff can sometimes forgo the niceties of professional decorum in the heat of the moment. I remember coming home in tears, overwhelmed by the harshness of the workspace. It was then my husband reminded me, "You're not a student anymore. You're not obliged to accept inappropriate behaviour. Stand up for yourself. If someone is used to giving harsh words, it's your place to let them know you won't accept it." This was a turning point. Allowing someone to diminish your dignity sends a signal to others that it's acceptable behaviour. But remember, allowing disrespect doesn't just reflect on them but shapes how you're perceived and treated by everyone else.

It's essential to understand that your reaction to such situations speaks volumes. Over-compliance or a continual attempt to appease someone who disrespects you doesn't just affect your peace of mind; it defines your professional persona. This isn't merely about personal comfort; it's about crafting a reputation that will carry you forward in your career, opening doors to new connections and opportunities.

Thus, if you find yourself simply enduring, hoping things will get better, let me offer a gentle reminder: **change doesn't happen on its own. It requires you to take action, to assertively draw your lines, and to communicate clearly and respectfully where those boundaries lie.** More than confrontation, it's about maintaining professional integrity and ensuring your work environment respects and reflects your values. As veteran actress Liz Smith says, **"Begin somewhere. You cannot build a reputation on what you intend to do."**

MAKING A CHANGE

If you're at a crossroads in your professional life, eager to shed the remnants of the past and embrace a new future, why stay tethered to any toxic relationship, be it personal or professional? After all, your career is a significant part of your identity. It deserves your full engagement and effort.

Ask yourself if your work environment truly supports your growth. If not, perhaps it's time to recalibrate those boundaries. After all, isn't it better to shape the environment around you than to let it shape you into someone you're not? As author Paul F. Davis says, **"If you don't feel it, flee from it. Go where you are celebrated, not merely tolerated."**

Moving ahead in your professional world is like sailing across a vast ocean. At times, you'll encounter tranquil waters, making progress feel effortless. Other times, you face fierce storms of bias or discrimination. It's in these tougher moments where your chance to shine emerges. Just as a skilled sailor uses the wind, no matter how wild, to her advantage, you too can harness these challenges as forces for growth and empowerment.

If it is a toxic work environment that tests your professional resilience, it can feel like being stuck in quicksand, where every move sinks you deeper. Remember, **while transformation is also a formidable option, exiting might also be a viable escape.**

Embracing change in your career doesn't have to be daunting. Think of it as a dance, where each new step, even if unfamiliar, teaches you a new rhythm. By maintaining an open mind, focusing on what you can control, and pursuing ongoing development, you transform potential obstacles into opportunities for growth.

Learn to develop a growth mindset and push yourself to step out of your comfort zone, be it through learning new skills or setting ambitious goals. You can turn potential pitfalls into progress. Mistakes, far from being setbacks, are stepping stones that enrich our adaptability and resilience.

In essence, you need to thrive in your professional life by using strategic foresight and unwavering commitment to growth. It's about taking charge of your career narrative and ensuring each step forward is taken with confidence and clarity. Are you ready to take the helm?

CHANGING CAREERS TO PURSUE DREAMS

Each thread that forms our career represents choices, aspirations, and sometimes, the harsh realities of workplace challenges. Yet, if the fabric of your professional life feels worn or misaligned with who you are, it might be time to consider a change. When you are ready to move forward, initiate such a transformation that it aligns perfectly with your personal aspirations and values.

So, for those of you feeling stagnant in your current roles, convinced that things might improve someday, it's crucial to realise that change often requires proactive steps. You must draw your boundaries, advocate for your worth, and decide if the environment you're in today will truly lead to the fulfilment you seek tomorrow. But if you find yourself consistently undervalued, if the recognition and opportunities you deserve are perpetually out of reach, then ask yourself: Who is saving the best piece of the pie for you?

Remember, **inertia can be comforting, but it's also a silent thief of potential**. If your current workplace doesn't fully utilise your skills or provide the growth you crave, it might be time to reassess. A fulfilling career should not only offer financial rewards but also utilise your talents and offer opportunities for advancement. Reflect on this: even high-ranking officials and respected diplomats sometimes choose to step away from prestigious positions because they don't find personal satisfaction.

Many of us endure less-than-ideal job conditions, holding on for the promise of future financial stability, like a pension or other benefits. But one has to wonder, is it really wise to spend the best years of your life in dissatisfaction, merely banking on the hope of comfort in your later years? Perhaps it's not. If your job feels more like a trap than something that makes you happy, fulfilled and valued, then let this be your sign to reevaluate it.

I realised this from the case of a professor of paediatrics, who, at sixty-two—just three years shy of retirement—was diagnosed with end-stage ovarian cancer. Sadly, we lost her shortly after. Her situation forced me to reconsider the true cost of clinging to a job solely for the pension, especially when there's no guarantee you'll ever get to enjoy those benefits. Why drag yourself through a career that doesn't bring you joy, for a future that isn't promised? Life doesn't always wait for our plans to unfold. Sometimes, you have to take a risk for immediate happiness and fulfilment. You have the power to change the trajectory of your career and your life.

Remember that choosing wisely doesn't just apply to battles. It also means knowing when to walk away from something that no longer serves you. It's about recognising that every workplace has its pulse. So, changing its rhythm might require more than just your effort. Sometimes, it might require a new environment.

Thus, if you're contemplating a career change or want to follow your dreams, view it as an act of courage that is your worth and potential. Embrace the possibility of a career that not only meets your needs but also challenges you to grow and thrive.

You can try the following steps to begin your new journey:

- Reassess Your Current Skills and Goals

  List your achievements, both professional and personal, and consider how these can be transferred into new career opportunities. This is a powerful exercise to recognise your own growth and potential, framing your career not just as a job but as a part of your personal evolution.

- Network Strategically

  Networking can often be overwhelming. So connect within specific industries or with professionals who align with your aspirations. Join professional groups on LinkedIn or even reach out to old colleagues. Each interaction should be a step towards your larger career goals.

- Consider Part-time or Flexible Roles

  For those balancing personal commitments with professional aspirations, part-time roles or flexible working options can be invaluable. Such arrangements can shelp maintain a career trajectory without sacrificing your personal life balance. They can also help you learn a skill that might lead to your dreams

- Continue Learning and Upskilling

  Sign up for courses that enhance your existing skills or develop new ones relevant to your desired field. If the prospect of stepping back to learning is daunting, look for online courses that can make education more accessible to you. Upskilling not only makes your profile more attractive to potential employers, but it can also give you the much-needed confidence and skills to pursue entrepreneurship.

CONCLUSION:

It's baffling to see many remain in stagnant, toxic work environments just to secure a comfortable pension. The years spent in these settings are often at the expense of youth and midlife vitality. If your job brings happiness, growth, and a pension, that's wonderful. But if it sacrifices your best years for mere financial security, it's worth rethinking your professional life. Now is the time to act, before energy wanes and market relevance fades.

As we draw this chapter to a close, let's reflect on how our careers intertwine with our broader lives. The journey to harmonise career ambitions with personal life is about achieving balance and integrating our professional endeavours into a larger, more holistic vision of what we want our lives to be.

Remember, a career that aligns with your deepest values and desires is a source of fulfilment and pride that extends beyond the office walls.

Encourage yourself to view career decisions not just in terms of potential gains or losses on the professional front but as choices that shape your entire life's narrative. As you contemplate these decisions, consider how they impact all facets of your life. Does this career path allow you to grow intellectually and emotionally? Does it give you enough time with your loved ones? Does it enable you to pursue personal projects and interests that light up your spirit? These questions are vital as they help you build a career that complements your life, not complicates it.

Here's to making choices that lead to a fulfilling and harmonious life!

Chapter 7

PRINCIPLE 5: MASTER YOUR MONEY – FINANCIAL EMPOWERMENT

"Give a woman a dollar, and she can put it to good use. Teach her about how money really works, and she can change the world."

— Linda Davis Taylor

So far, we've explored the concepts of self-realisation and self-reliance extensively. But it's important to understand that there's no true self-reliance without financial independence. What value does freedom have if one is financially tethered to another for even the most basic needs? The rule is simple yet harsh: if it's their money, then it's likely to be their rules, too. At this stage in life, many find themselves evaluating their financial journey, measuring the dreams of their youth against their current financial realities. With future needs like a dream home yet to be built, children's education, and perhaps mounting medical bills for ageing parents (especially if they didn't secure good insurance policies, the financial pressure can be immense). And let's not forget about the escalating healthcare costs that inevitably come with ageing.

For those who have been tirelessly chasing a 9-to-7 routine, lost in the daily hustle of only successfully accomplishing daily errands without pausing to realise how money flows in and out, it's a moment to pause and reflect. Many of us continue to soldier on day by day, waiting for a 'big day' that may never come. If such a day were destined to happen, wouldn't it have by now?(mostly, unless you are determined to make it happen now onwards)

At this phase of your life, it's important to pause and have a reality check, assimilate what you've achieved so far, and then move forward with a clear awareness of your current standing. You need to understand where you stand today so you can leap confidently into tomorrow.

Gone are the days when our parents viewed their children as bank accounts or fixed deposits. There's absolutely nothing wrong with investing everything in our children's education and upbringing. In fact, I was raised with the same values. But, if there's an alternative that allows for a little self-investment, then why not explore it?

We should learn to balance our commitment to our family with our own financial independence. It's the only way to ensure that we all thrive together. Why should you burden your children with financial responsibilities in your later years if you can take a few wise decisions today to ensure your financial independence?

For those like me who feel as financially literate as I once felt, believe me, mastering the basics isn't as hard as it seems. The world today overflows with information, making it easier than ever to educate ourselves. I started with *Let's Talk Money* by Monika Halan to get my basics right. Then, I took a more active role in managing my finances by connecting with a Chartered Accountant I truly trust. Remember, you need to seek help from the people you can trust. Find an experienced, trustworthy professional to help you if that's what you need.

For instance, my advisers are Mr. Mayank Agarwal and his wife, Mrs. Surbhi Agarwal, both finance graduates. Their expertise not only secures my financial future but enriches this book, offering you practical insights into managing your finances with acumen. They have generously outlined a framework for effective financial management that I am eager to share with you readers.

In a world clamouring for women's empowerment, especially in India where the urban educated class is vocal about it, I've had the opportunity to see its true colours through personal experience. Post-graduation, I married into a family where, unlike my childhood home where my mother managed the household finances while my father was the breadwinner, my mother-in-law was the primary financial contributor.

This was a revelation. While my mother managed finances efficiently and kept my father worry-free about daily expenses and savings, stepping into a household where a woman was not just managing but earning the bulk of the family's income, opened my eyes to what female financial independence truly means. Financial independence means having the ability and resources to survive independently. In India, where a significant portion of women might not feel the urgency to be financially independent, they continue to struggle for basic rights, including access to healthcare. You need to understand that empowerment starts with the ability to sustain oneself financially, without which freedom is just an illusion. As artist Rebeca Mojica rightly says, **"Being financially independent means having the power to make your own choices and live life on your own terms."**

In my consultations, I frequently encounter patients whose healthcare choices, such as pregnancy check-ups and delivery locations, are dictated not by their own needs but by their in-laws who hold the financial reins. These decisions, which are often pivotal to a woman's health and well-being, become transactions dictated by financial power rather than medical necessity. For instance, when a woman prefers to deliver at a better-equipped facility to mitigate risks, she is sometimes met with threats from her in-laws, who are unwilling to bear the additional costs. This dynamic is not just about healthcare but reflects a broader issue of financial control and independence within family structures.

In most families, the in-laws are emotionally detached from their new daughters-in-law. Even if they show attachment, it could be out of social pressures or because of the bride's parents. In many families, financial independence is withheld, and women are made to rely on their in-laws or husbands for money, even for crucial matters like healthcare. It's a stark reminder that without financial independence, claiming any form of personal independence remains a challenge. In a world where financial means often dictate choices and opportunities, the lack of control over one's finances can severely limit one's freedom and decision-making power.

Here's how Mr. Mayank Agarwal, my ever-enthusiastic Chartered Accountant, who handles every penny of what I earn and invest, explains the need for financial planning.

"Midlife," he begins with a sparkle in his eye, "is not just a time to reflect on past achievements and challenges. It's a launching pad for securing your future."

He lays out a financial road map with six major steps for those of us who need some support and guidance to start our journey to financial independence.

ASSESS AND SET GOALS

Let's dive into a topic we often avoid until it unexpectedly pops up: financial health. Think about setting up a yearly financial check-up. This screening should involve examining your income, spending, taxes, assets, investments, and debts. Retirement might feel very distant to you now, but it'll arrive before you know it. So, instead of stressing about the future, just start preparing for it. Planning ahead can turn retirement into that long-awaited break you've always promised yourself. So, start planning right away.

Assess if your savings are ready to support your dream retirement. Adjusting your contributions now can make all the difference later. Tweak those monthly savings a bit and make long-term investments for your future. Think of it as adjusting your diet as you age. It's necessary and, honestly, quite beneficial.

The next step is to prioritise your short-term goals. It could be your children's education or, upgrading your family's car or renovating your house. Set investment goals and timelines for each of these ideas so that you get a better grip on your money. Get your CA's help and make smart investments for short and mid-term so that you can focus on your present life and your future goals without stress,

If your emergency fund and short-term goals are ready, then take a look at those dreams gathering dust in your mind. What is it that you always wanted? Sketch out your ambitions for the next decade. It will help you understand and invest for the long term. Setting clear financial targets will keep you from wandering aimlessly and ensures every step is purposeful.

You might think of managing your money as about crunching numbers. In truth, it is more about making those numbers work for you, ensuring they pave a path to the life you desire. This reminds me of something singer Reba McEntire said about money: "I think every woman should have financial independence, but it's not just for the money. It's for the security and the power that comes with it."

Get your finances in order, because life is too short to live it on anyone else's terms but our own.

CONQUER DEBT

When it comes to managing debt, imagine you're at a lavish buffet. Everything looks tempting, but you know not everything on that table is good for you. Here's how you can smartly fill your plate without regretting it later:

- **Prioritise and Pay Off**

  At the buffet, you'd probably start with the dish that you crave but might run out soon. Similarly, in your financial journey, start with the high-interest debts. They're like the priciest dish at the buffet, costing you more the longer you let them sit on your plate. Tackling these first not only reduces the cost over time but also gives you a psychological win that can motivate you to handle smaller debts with more confidence.

- **Avoid New Debt**

  It might look tempting to add a new shiny credit card or loan to your wallet, but it's just going to weigh you down. Better to walk past and pat yourself on the back for showing restraint. New debt is like an extra dessert; you enjoy it now but will regret it later when you're trying to 'work it off'.

- **Explore Consolidation**

  This is like turning two half-eaten dishes into one full meal that actually tastes better. Consolidating your debts can streamline what you owe, possibly with a nicer side of lower interest rates, making your financial management less of a juggling act. It's about creating a more manageable and appetising financial meal that you can tackle with gusto.

- **Limit EMIs**

  EMIs can be sneaky little things, like those tiny appetisers that don't look like much but add up before you know it. If it's not something you absolutely need, maybe think twice about buying it on instalment. Consider each EMI as a commitment to a set of extra bites you'll have to chew over the coming months or even years; opting out when it's not necessary keeps your financial plate cleaner.

- **Wise Credit Card Usage**

  Use your credit card sparingly and wisely, like a good seasoning. Make sure you clear the slate every month to avoid the extra 'flavour' of interest. It's about enjoying the convenience without overindulging. Just like seasoning enhances a dish, wise credit card use can enhance your financial health without overwhelming it.

Just as with a good meal, managing your finances well can leave you feeling satisfied, not stuffed. So, take control, make smart choices, and watch your financial health improve bite by bite. This approach not only keeps your debt levels healthy but also bolsters your overall financial resilience.

BOOST YOUR INCOME

In life, we often get used to our financial and career routines without much thought. This section is an invitation to take a step back and think differently. Most women feel too tied to their jobs and don't focus on diversifying and looking for better opportunities to make more money. I think it's because society generally tends to vilify women who are driven to make money. In our society, women are encouraged to make money only to support their husbands while ensuring it doesn't bruise their egos.

To such women, I implore that we should make choices that not only improve our bank balances but also enrich our daily lives. Keep an eye out for better opportunities to make money.

If you still need some motivation, turn to author Stephen Covey's words, **"Your economic security does not lie in your job; it lies in your own power to produce – to think, to learn, to create, to adapt."**

Let's turn ordinary financial decisions into opportunities for personal growth and financial health.

- **Career Evolution**

  Pause for a moment and think about where you stand in your career. Do you find your job fulfilling? Does it excite you every morning? If not, perhaps it's time to try a new path. You can start small with a different project or try a different skill. More than climbing the career ladder, it's about ensuring that your career genuinely makes you happy.

- **Look for Side Hustle Opportunities**

  Whether it's painting, writing, or crafting, these activities can morph into more than just hobbies. They can provide a supplemental income and, more importantly, immense personal satisfaction.

- **Invest Wisely**

  Consider your investments as you would your closest relationships. Choose with care, nurture with patience, and plan it for long-term enrichment. Begin with ventures you comprehend and resonate with your risk appetite. This approach will not only secure your future but also grant you peace of mind.

- **Negotiate Your Salary**

Reflect on your current role and contributions. Are they adequately recognised and compensated? If not, prepare to step forward and advocate for what you deserve. Understand your worth, articulate your accomplishments, and negotiate not just for a salary increment but for what symbolises respect and recognition of your efforts.

- **Freelance or Consult**

If your expertise is a well from which many have drawn, consider offering it as a freelance service or consulting. This shift can allow you to control your time, choose your projects, and meet your professional and personal goals on your terms.

- **Rent Out Assets**

Look around you; resources that lie idle could be avenues for additional income. Whether it's an empty room, a seldom-used car, or old equipment, these assets can be transformed into profitable ventures with little effort.

- **Online Earning Potential**

If you have a skill, a product, or knowledge to share, platforms online can help you reach an audience that is already seeking what you offer. The digital world is vast and filled with opportunities and you can seek them with minimal risks. Dive into this digital marketplace with an open heart and a strategic mind.

In embracing these strategies, remember that it's not just about enhancing your financial standing but about enriching your life, nurturing your passions, and rediscovering the joys of your professional and personal endeavours.

SAVE AND INVEST STRATEGICALLY

Let's dive into some tactics to strengthen your financial health because, let's be honest, surprises are fantastic at parties but not on your bank statements:

- **Get insurance coverage**

  Life can throw some serious curveballs, and there's no dodging them. Your best bet is to be prepared. Arm yourself with insurance—life, health, and property. These will serve as your safety net, offering not just peace of mind but a financial umbrella for those rainy days.

- **Prioritise making an emergency fund**

  Stashing away enough money to cover three to six months of expenses is a wise strategy. Just make sure this fund is easily accessible, like in a savings account or short-term debt funds, ready for you to tap into during unexpected moments.

- **Take advantage of tax benefits**

  Planning ahead with investments in PPF, EPF, NPS, and tax-saving FDs can lighten your tax load and **enhance your savings over the long haul.**

- **Buy gold**

  In every Indian household, gold is like the treasured heirloom from grandma—valued and handed down through generations. It's a solid defence against inflation and a shiny buffer in shaky times. Treat it as a long-term asset; patience pays off.

- **Get into equity investments**

  If you have some extra money, why not explore the stock market? It will be full of ups and downs, but the chance for significant gains is enticing. Putting money into mutual funds, stocks, and ETFs might turn out to be quite profitable with time.

- **Invest in real estate**

  Investing in real estate demands patience and time, but once it starts to pay off, whether through rental income or through sale, the benefits can be substantial. Be sure to do thorough research and pick a spot that's expected to develop.

- **Consult a financial adviser**

  Stepping into the investment world can seem overwhelming, especially if you've always been taught to save rather than invest. A financial adviser can simplify the complex, offer advice tailored to your situation, and help you navigate your investment choices. Talking to a professional is a wise move to start your investment journey on the right foot.

PLAN FOR HEALTHCARE

Let's make sure everything clicks in terms of securing your financial health. After all, surprises are best left for birthday parties, not your financial statements.

- **Review Your Insurance Coverage**

  Check up on your health insurance like you'd check the oil in your car; regularly and with intention. With healthcare costs not playing nice, ensure you're well-covered not only for the big emergencies but also the smaller, regular health checks and treatments. Cover all your bases—your kids, your partner, and especially if you have elderly parents.

- **Explore Long-Term Care Options**

  With time, the chances of needing steady medical care creep up. Don't let health issues sneak up on you. Planning for long-term care ensures your later years are golden. Look into insurance that covers home care or assisted living—think of it as a nest egg for your health.

- **Prioritise Wellness**

  Routine health check-ups? They're your early detection system. Living a healthy lifestyle is about bettering your life day by day. Simple activities like daily walks, joining a local gym, or a yoga session can significantly uplift your well-being. Manage stress with practices like meditation not only for peace of mind but for a healthier life down the road.

Taking these steps is about investing in a healthier, fuller life for you and your loved ones.

BUILD YOUR LEGACY

Drafting a will and keeping it current is crucial. Let me explain why.

- **Create a Comprehensive Will**

  Drafting a will is your way of ensuring that the things you've worked hard for end up in the right hands after you're gone. It's about taking responsibility for your assets and making sure there's no confusion or conflict among those you care about. Especially in a place like India, where family relationships can be intricate, a clear and detailed will is key to maintaining harmony. Think of it as your final gesture of care—a guide you leave behind to safeguard your legacy and protect your family.

- **Review Regularly**

  Your will shouldn't be something you write and forget. Life changes—marriages, the birth of children, and new possessions mean your will should change too. Updating your will during significant life events ensures it reflects your current situation and desires. It's akin to renovating your home to suit new needs or preferences; your will requires periodic updates to accurately mirror the state of your life.

  By diligently creating and updating your will, you provide peace and certainty to your loved ones, making sure your wishes are understood and your legacy is honoured while your estate is managed. This is how you continue to look after your family, even when you're not around.

SEEK PROFESSIONAL GUIDANCE

So, how can you stick to your financial goals and keep your money plans up to date as your life evolves?

- **Talk to your Financial Adviser**

  Get advice from a financial adviser as they can break down complex investment choices, explain the ins and outs of tax rules, and point out any risks. Especially in India, where most people don't have enough knowledge about smart investing, having a financial expert by your side can make a huge difference. They'll help you handle your investments well and make plans for your future with confidence.

- **Check in Regularly**

  Schedule appointments with your financial adviser to go over your finances. These check-ins will allow you to tweak your financial strategies to match your current situation and future dreams.

  By working with a financial adviser and making regular reviews a habit, you can manage your finances more clearly.

CONCLUSION:

By making informed decisions, let us get closer to a future where we are truly free — free to dream, to act, and to live on our own terms. As we wrap up this chapter, let's remember the impact financial independence can have, especially for women. Philanthropist Melinda Gates captured it best when she said, **"When money flows into the hands of women, who have the authority to use it, everything changes — for women, their families, and their communities."**

Chapter 8

PRINCIPLE 6: CHAMPION YOUR HEALTH – PRIORITISE HEALTH AND WELL-BEING

"When health is absent, wisdom cannot reveal itself, art cannot manifest, strength cannot fight, wealth becomes useless, and intelligence cannot be applied."

— Herophilus

If you're not healthy in your mid-thirties and forties, then yes, you definitely need to be damn scared. By now, life has surely taught you that in most circumstances (we'll ignore the miracles), we get water from where we dig. We usually don't harvest what we didn't sow. So, if you were never the athletic type of person who has been hitting the gym since eighteen, like me, then please, dear readers, ignore all the chapters of this book you've read so far. Pull out the pages of this chapter and paste them right at the beginning. Even the Constitution of India grants you the right to health as your fundamental right. There can be no conversation about you asking anyone else's permission to stay healthy, and if it's because you've been ignoring your health, then please, reposition your glasses and read this chapter.

PHYSICAL HEALTH

My pregnancies were physically challenging, limiting my capacity and endurance. For the first time in my life, I felt what it must be like for the elderly when your body doesn't match your mental frequency. Honestly, I couldn't pursue physical training sessions like my husband, who cannot miss his morning sessions for any reason known to mankind. I was never regular, for all the popular reasons we're all aware of. But believe me, when I entered my mid-forties, my musculoskeletal system started telling me that age is not just a number. That's when I began to take my workout sessions seriously, and now I don't feel the pain in my thigh muscles, knee joints, and hip joints; they're all minding their behaviour. The perimenopausal symptoms of muscle pains, joint pains, lack of sleep and vigour, the hot flashes, the irritability—all seem to take care of themselves. I certainly advise everyone out there to please get a health check-up done (this part was easy for me because I'm a doctor myself, and my husband is a physician). Get your physical fitness card and carve out that forty-minute slot five times a week for yourself.

My patients often ask me, "You're on your toes the entire day, so do you really need to go to the gym or cycle that much?" My simple answer to them is: You can see me working from 5 a.m. to 11 p.m. only because I spend that 40 minutes in the morning preparing my physical machinery for the long days that I work. Here's a simple tip for all those people who believe that doing household chores all day means they don't need any muscle training: Your fat is like your savings account; it's about how much you put in and how much you save (and I'm not talking about any medical disorder affecting your metabolism). Our bodies are almost eighty per cent of what we eat and twenty per cent of what we spend.

So, as I started taking my workouts seriously, I realised that **maintaining physical health boils down to focusing on three key aspects: aerobic activities, strength training, and flexibility and balance.**

Aerobic Activities:

Let's think about movement as something more than just exercise—it's a way to enrich our lives daily. Take walking, for instance. It's simple, right?

But oh, how profound its effects can be. Walking builds your stamina, strengthens your legs, and helps fend off bone issues like osteoporosis. Whether you're weaving through your neighbourhood solo or chatting with a friend, targeting 8,000 to 10,000 steps each day can really elevate your health.

Now, let's float over to swimming. Imagine it as a kind sanctuary for your body. It gives you a solid workout—burning calories, strengthening your heart, enhancing your muscles—all while the water cradles you gently. This is exercise that doesn't feel like a chore but more like a retreat.

And if you're looking to sprinkle some joy into your routine, why not dance? Dancing lifts your heart rate, boosts your balance, and increases your flexibility. It's a celebration of your body's abilities and a fun twist on the usual workout.

Investing in these activities—be it a gym, yoga classes, or cycling—is investing in your well-being. Even a bike ride in the morning can kickstart your day with energy and fresh air.

But here's a key point to remember: real improvements in your body come from consistent, regular effort. You might think that running around the house all day counts as active, but it's the continuous, heart-pumping activities that really count. House chores might make you feel busy, but they don't quite get your heart rate up like a brisk walk or a swim does.

Strength Training is Non-Negotiable

As we grow older, keeping muscle mass is a bit like trying to hold water in your hands—challenging but crucial. Strength training is essential here. It's not about lifting massive weights or building visible muscles; it's about maintaining the strength around your vital joints and back to support your body's frame as you age. You might wonder, "Why bother with muscles at this age?" Well, keeping these muscles strong is about easing the load on your joints, perhaps even delaying the need for more drastic measures like joint replacements.

If this sounds daunting, consider getting a trainer who can guide you. Start with light weights and simple exercises. As you grow stronger, you can gradually increase the challenge. You'll be amazed at the positive changes in your body and overall life quality.

Flexibility and Balance are Essential

Keeping your body flexible and balanced becomes increasingly important as you age. Yoga can be a wonderful aid here. It stretches and strengthens not just your body but also calms your mind and keeps your heart healthy. Tai chi is another gentle yet powerful way to maintain balance and ease joint pain. Pilates is excellent for strengthening your core and keeping you limber, which becomes essential as the years roll on.

Incorporating these practices into your life doesn't just improve your physical health—they enrich your entire being, making every day more vibrant and full of potential.

DIET

If you're anything like me, you might remember a time when you could eat whatever you fancied and easily work it off. Well, my friend, those days are in the rearview mirror because midlife has arrived, and it's brought some new rules for what we put on our plates. Why the change? Our bodies, which once let us indulge in those late-night binges, are now asking for a bit more consideration. As we age, our basic metabolic rate (the energy we burn for basic functions like breathing and keeping our hearts beating) slows down. Our heart rate and physical activity levels drop, too. This means our bodies need less fuel than before. So it's important to watch what you eat and how much you eat. For instance, if you used to eat two chapatis at each meal without a second thought, hitting fifty might change the game. Those same two chapatis could now lead to some surprising weight gain.

Now, let's explore a few simple yet impactful tweaks you can make to your diet without driving yourself crazy.

- **Boost Your Calcium Intake and Don't Forget About Vitamin D**

Calcium really steps into the spotlight when it comes to bone health, doesn't it? Picture this: after menopause, it feels like your body is grabbing calcium with both hands, holding onto it like the last piece of sweet kheer at a feast. But why does this shift happen? Well, as our oestrogen takes a bit of a retreat, our bones get a bit more vulnerable. So, what's our move here? It's pretty straightforward—ramp up on calcium-rich foods. Sprinkle some extra curd into your diet, pour yourself a comforting glass of milk, or slice up some paneer. And if seafood is on your menu, sardines are a gem—tiny bones included because they're packed with goodness. You don't need to flip your diet on its head; just nudge in a bit more calcium. Believe me, your bones will show their gratitude.

Then there's Vitamin D, without which calcium might just wander aimlessly in your body. How do you reel in enough Vitamin D? Catch some early sun rays as you sip your morning tea. This vitamin also tags along in foods like fish, egg yolks, and liver—simple sources to tap into.

And if you're exploring a vegan journey, keep an eye out for those crucial nutrients often found in animal products. For all women, especially as you edge towards menopause, keep tabs on your iron levels. Unchecked, this can sneak into anaemia territory, particularly if your menstrual periods throw you curveballs. Let's not forget that during the first few years of menopause, your calcium stores take a hit. It's crucial, then, to stay attuned to your body's signals and keep up with those health check-ups.

- **Load Up on Whole Grains**

Step aside, refined grains; whole grains are where it's at. Swap in some whole wheat for your roti, or opt for brown rice. These grains aren't just filling; they're brimming with nutrients that help keep your digestion smooth and your weight in check—essential as your metabolism begins to take it easy. Whole grains are like cheerleaders for a happy gut, and a happy gut means a happier you.

- **Lean Proteins Are Your Best Friend**

  With the years ticking by, muscle mass might start to play hide and seek, while fat seems to find a favourite spot to settle. Here's where lean proteins make an entrance. Dal, grilled fish, paneer tikka—these aren't just tasty; they're muscle-maintenance heroes. They help fire up your metabolism, too. Throw in some regular physical activity, and you're all set to keep those muscles around.

- **Don't be afraid of Healthy Fats**

  Now, let's clear the air about fats. They're not all villains. In fact, healthy fats—like those in avocados, nuts, seeds, and yes, our good old desi ghee—are heart-healthy and vital for hormone balance, especially handy during menopause. So go on, add a splash of olive oil to your salad or a dab of ghee on your paratha. It's good for you, and it makes everything taste better.

- **Limit Processed Foods and Added Sugars**

  Processed foods and added sugars are like those fair-weather friends who love to stir up trouble. They can mess with your weight and blood pressure and even amplify those menopause symptoms. Try to keep them at arm's length. Lean towards whole, unprocessed foods that nourish you without the fuss. Craving something sweet? A piece of natural jaggery can hit the spot without sending your sugar levels soaring.

MENTAL AND EMOTIONAL WELL-BEING

Let's explore what's unfolding in the quieter corners of your life—your mind and heart. It's not just our bodies that crave nourishment and strength; our mental and emotional wellness is equally vital. So, while you're busy fortifying your bones with calcium and fuelling up with whole grains, have you thought about how to shield your mind from the day's stresses or soothe the anxiety that tends to linger after the sun sets?

- **Stress and Anxiety Management**

Imagine stress as an uninvited guest at a party. One minute, you're handling everything smoothly; the next, you're on the edge over something small, like an unwashed cup. Stress and anxiety don't have to dominate your days. There are ways to manage them without hiding in a corner with a tub of ice cream (though let's be honest, that's a solid plan on some days). Mindfulness practices like meditation and yoga will help you stay calm, breathe a little easier, and keep you emotionally balanced, even when life decides to go full-on Bollywood drama on you.

Keeping your mind sharp is like tending to a vibrant garden. Have you ever walked into a room and forgotten why? It's a little nudge reminding us that our mental space needs upkeep, too. Engage in activities that challenge your brain, like solving a puzzle with your morning tea or diving into a good book. Maybe start a new hobby that sparks your curiosity—knitting, perhaps? Imagine gifting hand-knitted scarves next Diwali—what a delightful thought to keep your spirits high and mind engaged!

Finally, don't forget the power of staying socially active. It will keep you open to new people and perspectives and will only help you grow. Midlife can get lonely, especially when the kids are off living their lives and your friends are knee-deep in their own issues. But staying connected is key to keeping your emotional well-being intact. Invite friends over for pakoras, join a kitty party, or just have a good old-fashioned phone chat with a loved one. You can also have a weekly chai session with your neighbour, join a bhajan group or travel group, or volunteer at the local mandir—these connections are what keep you grounded. Reach out, connect, and remember that you're part of a bigger community. Keeping your brain engaged and your social circle buzzing is just as important as those morning walks in the park.

- **Practicing Mindfulness**

Mindfulness isn't about sitting still, adorned in silence; it's about engaging fully with the present moment. Whether you're savouring your morning tea, listening to a favourite melody, or feeling the texture of the air around you, mindfulness allows us to press pause on life's fast-forward button. It's a simple practice that brings profound joy and tranquillity to our everyday hustle.

So, how do you start? There are simple, everyday techniques that can bring a sense of calm and clarity to your life and can help you stay grounded, connected, and at peace, no matter what the day throws at you.

- **Breathing Exercises**

Sometimes, our inner turmoil mirrors rush-hour chaos. A few deep breaths can clear the mind, like choosing a quieter route on a busy day. Sit back, inhale deeply, hold for a moment, then exhale slowly—letting go of the day's tensions. It's a quick fix that also builds long-term peace. If you want to take it up a notch, try pranayama, the practice of breath control. Techniques like Anulom Vilom (alternate nostril breathing) or Bhramari (humming bee breath) can help you centre yourself and bring peace to even the busiest of days.

- **Guided Meditation**

If the thought of quiet meditation daunts you, consider guided meditation like having a compassionate guide leading you through a busy street. Find a comfortable spot, press play on a meditation app, and let a calming voice shepherd you through relaxation and introspection. It's a supportive way to find peace amidst the hustle of life.

- **Body Scan**

Consider a body scan as a method to decompress after a long day. Lie down, close your eyes, and gently traverse your body from toe to head. Release any stored tension, like loosening a tightly wound thread. It's a profound reset for both mind and body.

- **Mindful Communication**

Most of us have multiple lines of thought running through our minds. We've all been there, nodding along in a conversation while mentally running through the week's grocery list. As you drive to work, you might be thinking of a gift you need to buy, your daughter's school project, and an upcoming work appointment, all while battling traffic. You might talk, vent, and rant a lot, but do you actually communicate? Do you pay a hundred percent attention to what someone else is saying?

The next time you're chatting with someone, whether it's your neighbour about the latest gossip in the colony or your spouse discussing the rising prices of petrol, try being fully present. This might actually give you some respite from all the noise in your mind and help you communicate your needs better. You'll be amazed at how these small moments of connection can strengthen your relationships.

- **Journalling**

The best way to make sense of the jumble of thoughts in your head is to put pen to paper. Journalling is a powerful tool for anyone who's trying to process their emotions and clear their mind. Grab a notebook and start writing. Don't worry about grammar or making it perfect; just let the words flow like a stream. Sometimes, when you see your thoughts on paper, especially angry thoughts, you'll feel that they're more manageable now that you've expressed them in a healthy way without hurting anyone or misdirecting them. It will help you understand and process your triggers. Are you angry at your son for watching TV on loud volume, or are you angry that your partner is not helping you with your mental load?

Journalling will help you untangle your thoughts and reconnect with an idea you've always wanted to try or a dream you had forgotten long ago. Some people use journals exclusively for gratitude, noting down the things they're grateful for. They say the practice helps you become more positive in life. Others use journalling as a medium to vent out their negative issues, while some use it as a place for brainstorming. Journalling can be especially helpful if you don't have a nonjudgmental and receptive listener in your life. You might find that by the end of it, you've not only untangled your thoughts but also gained some surprising insights into your own mind.

CONSISTENCY AND ROUTINE

We all start a new practice with the best intentions. Think of all those New Year's resolutions to eat more salads, which end up forgotten by mid-January, replaced by comforting plates of aloo parathas. It's the same with everything else, too. Making changes is easy, but sticking to them is the tough part. Consistency and discipline are the only answers to this issue.

- **Exercise Consistency**

  We all know we should be moving more and eating better, but knowing and doing are two very different things. It's like buying all the ingredients for a healthy, nutritious meal and then ordering out because you're too tired to cook. The key here is to make both exercise and healthy eating a habit—something you do without even thinking. More than motivation, habit-building is what will help you make sustainable changes.

  It is recommended that an adult should do 150 minutes of moderate aerobic activity per week. This may sound intimidating, but if you break it down, that's just 30 minutes a day, five days a week. It doesn't sound too bad now, does it? Whether it's a brisk walk through the park while you listen to some songs or doing a few squats while waiting for your tea to boil, it's a good place to start. It can make a difference. The trick is to keep it small but regular until you build the habit.

  The same goes for your eating habits. Don't expect to change your and your family's eating habits overnight. It will take time to bring in substantial changes. You need to focus on balance and moderation. Keep your meals regular and your portions sensible. Don't immediately cut out your favourite foods—just learn to enjoy them in smaller quantities. Remember that health doesn't glow up at the end of a diet. You need to practice your new habits throughout your life to sustain your good health and well-being.

- **Routine Health Check-ups**

Routine health check-ups are something we all tend to put off, like that cupboard we keep promising to organise. I know, I know, they might be as appealing as a visit to the in-laws on a Sunday afternoon for some of you. But here's the thing—you can't ignore them, hoping they'll magically disappear. Because both you and I know—they won't.

Another common error I see a lot of people committing is that if, God forbid, they get diagnosed with a chronic medical disorder like high blood pressure, abnormal sugar metabolism, or thyroid deficiency, they tend to go into self-denial and try to defer starting treatment. They fear that once they start taking medicines, they'll be bound to them forever. Or even worse, if they do start and their parameters improve, they stop the medications on their own, presuming the condition is cured.

Just a few humble explanations here. Please do not be scared of starting treatment. Remember, the medications prescribed have undergone thorough safety trials before they're available for human use. Second, it's not the medicine that harms your vital organs like your kidneys, heart, and blood vessels—it's the deranged biology that does. It's the high-pressure blood flowing to the kidneys that damages them, not that the kidneys interview the blood before it enters the renal artery to check if your pressure and sugar levels are naturally normal or under the influence of a drug. Please remember these vital organs are the end organs that merely face the brunt of deranged metabolism and biology. So please be kind to your body parts.

I urge you not to be scared of the tests, the diagnosis, or the treatment, but be damn scared of untreated or uncontrolled disease. That's the only thing to be scared of.

For women between the ages of 40 and 60, embracing regular health check-ups is not just a good idea—it's essential. Here's why these check-ups are needed:

- **Early Detection of Health Issues**

  Midlife can be full of surprises, and not all of them are pleasant. Your body may begin to introduce you to unexpected guests like heart disease, diabetes, or even cancer. Regular health screenings act as an early warning system, the kind we all wish we had for every aspect of life. From mammograms to cervical and uterine cancer screenings, these tests are crucial. They can catch problems when they're still in their early stages—manageable and not as menacing. Think of it as catching a smoulder before it turns into a full-blown kitchen fire. So, skipping these check-ups? It's not a wise option.

- **Monitoring Chronic Conditions**

  If you're already acquainted with chronic conditions like high blood pressure or diabetes, regular check-ups are your way of keeping tabs on these familiar foes. Consistent monitoring ensures that these conditions are managed effectively, helping prevent complications that can stem from them. It's about keeping things under control before they boil over, ensuring you stay as balanced and comfortable as possible.

- **Preventive Care**

  Routine check-ups are akin to preventive maintenance for your body, much like servicing your AC before the heat of summer hits. During these visits, your doctor isn't just looking for problems—they're also offering valuable advice tailored just for you. Maybe it's about tweaking your diet or encouraging more consistent exercise. These appointments are opportunities to make small, manageable changes that can head off larger issues down the road.

- **Building a Relationship with Healthcare Providers**

  Establishing a solid connection with a healthcare provider you trust and enjoy seeing regularly is key. Regular visits help build a strong bond, enabling open discussions about any changes or symptoms you observe. A great healthcare provider comprehends your history and unique health requirements, offering tailored guidance and assistance. Trusting your doctor enhances your commitment to their advice, reducing the urge to doubt every aspect or consult Dr. Google for every question.

- **Choosing the Right Doctor**

  Take the time to do your research and choose the right doctor for you. Once you've found someone you trust, try to avoid doubting their advice by cross-referencing everything online. Medical expertise is built upon years of study and practice, something no amount of Googling can replicate. Trust in their qualifications and experience. Focus your mental energy on your own projects and dreams—let the medical professionals handle your health.

CONCLUSION:

Midlife isn't a time to wind down. It's a chance to gear up for what's next! Sure, you might face some reminders of ageing, like creaky joints or mood swings, but remember, this period also brings a wealth of maturity and wisdom. Take charge of your health with confidence and clarity, knowing yourself better than ever. Make those healthcare appointments a priority, not just for survival, but to thrive in this dynamic phase of life. Trust me, your future self will thank you for it.

Chapter 9

PRINCIPLE 7: EMBRACE AUTHENTICITY – LIVE AUTHENTICALLY

"The privilege of a lifetime is to become who you truly are."

— Carl Jung

So far in the book, you've been on a journey of reevaluating and reassessing your current position, re-gauging where you stand to make the necessary corrections within you and around you, all to design your life the way you've imagined it or the way you want it. The focus has been on emphasising that you are the protagonist of your own story. The story continues as long as you do. There's always a new chapter to add as long as you don't give up. And more importantly, you need to realise that there is no story once the protagonist is gone. Every story is indeed a narrative of the protagonist's life, and when the protagonist dies, there might be one or two episodes that drag on, but the major part of the story ends.

Once you grasp that singular concept, you stop playing side characters in everyone else's stories. Instead, you learn to start writing your own script and begin weaving others into your narrative. You might argue, how can that change real life? Yes, it does. It changes your perception. It gives you the feeling of being in control rather than being controlled. It's almost like the narrative of the half-full or half-empty glass. Call it half-empty, and you'll crib; call it half-full, and there's contentment.

I recall a reunion with two of my friends from school. They were both homemakers who were discussing how they get their husbands to buy them nice sarees, jewellery, and their choice of furniture, all while letting the husbands and kids think they were the decision-makers. These women, fully aware of how tactfully they've led their families to get exactly what they wanted, were laughing their hearts out and called it mastering the art. Indeed, that's a win-win situation for everyone, where everyone believes they're the decision-makers. The women get what they want, the husbands feel magnanimous as givers and providers, satisfied that they're keeping the characters in their story happy, and the kids, well, they're invariably happy in a happy family. That's what's called striking a balance.

Now that you've decided to take the driver's seat and are prepared to navigate your path, you need to clearly know where you're headed. And you're no longer a school kid, so you also know how to gauge the responsibility of your actions. You can move ahead with your own rules. This is your canvas—create your picture and fill it with your own colours. Yet, I would still add a word of caution. Just as some of you feel the need to gauge the length of your stride, someone said to me, even while I was writing this book, "Be careful, Varuna, about advising anyone to make radical professional decisions." I replied that there was no need to worry, as at no point was I asking anyone to stop using common sense. For instance, if you wish to make a career shift, be sure of your professional skills, or if you're sure you want to move into a particular profession, you start working for it now. It's said in financial planning that wherever you wish to see yourself ten years from now, you have to start working on it now. This is what I've been insisting on all along. Know yourself, feel your dreams, and at least try to fulfil them once so you can die fulfilled.

Don't be scared to take up this journey for unnecessary reasons like the fear of being judged, the fear of failure, or the fear of not making it. Because now, it's not for anyone else that you wish to do something. You don't want to sing to become Lata Mangeshkar or dance to become Birju

Maharaj. Those are lifetime tapasyas, and yes, you might be late for that. But something in the way of your journey you've already traversed, and you've arrived. You want to sing because you want to sing. You want to dance because you want to dance. That's the beauty of having no pressure to prove, no fear of failing. Just being yourself. Just humming to yourself, just dancing to your tune, just being with yourself.

What Does It Mean to Be Authentic?

Let's start with a simple question: what does authenticity really mean? Think about the last time you did something that just felt right. Maybe it was standing up for yourself in a conversation or choosing to spend a quiet evening with a book instead of attending a social event because you needed that downtime. That's authenticity in action. It's about being deeply connected to who you truly are and making choices that align with that essence. It's a way of living where your actions reflect your inner beliefs, desires, and values.

WHY AUTHENTICITY MATTERS

Our world is overflowing with social pressures and often unrealistic expectations, which can make it challenging to consistently hold true to your authenticity.

- You might occasionally feel as though you're the only one struggling.

- Discovering others who share and understand your values can be difficult.

- As you forge your own path, there are moments when you might feel isolated from those around you.

- The push to conform can come from everywhere—friends, society, and even loved ones.

- There are times when blending in might seem far simpler than standing out.

- Remaining faithful to your passions and to your true self can often feel like an ongoing struggle.

So, why should we value authenticity so highly? When you're genuine, people notice. Picture yourself at a family gathering where, instead of just nodding along with every conversation, you express your own opinions calmly and honestly. It might surprise some people initially, but they'll soon come to respect you more for it. Authenticity fosters trust, which is priceless, whether it's with your family, colleagues, or friends, and particularly with yourself.

But the benefits of living authentically extend beyond gaining trust. It also makes you feel profoundly better. Reflect on those moments when you followed your instincts, even when the decision was tough, like quitting a well-paying yet unfulfilling job. It was probably frightening, but do you remember the relief you felt afterwards? That's because living in harmony with your true self brings a deep sense of peace and purpose. It's like the relief you feel when you finally take off a pair of uncomfortable shoes and slip into ones that fit perfectly.

HOW TO LIVE A MORE AUTHENTIC LIFE

- Begin by embracing honesty with yourself and others. Consider those times you might have skirted the truth to avoid conflict. How did you feel afterwards? Being honest is the foundation of living authentically. It's like choosing a nutritious home-cooked meal over quick junk food—it takes a bit more effort but is much better for you in the long run.

- Make it a point to fully express yourself. Have you ever kept quiet during a conversation and later wished you had spoken up? Being open and honest about your views is essential for authenticity. It takes courage and a deep appreciation for yourself to share your true thoughts, especially when it might be simpler to remain silent.

- Take time to identify what truly motivates you. Have you ever agreed to plans that didn't excite you just to keep others happy? Understanding your deepest desires lets you steer your life rather than simply tagging along for the ride. Imagine realising you'd much rather spend a quiet afternoon in a park with a good book than in a crowded mall—that's discovering what truly makes you tick.

- Address the stuff you've been putting off, whether it's that messy spot in your home or a friendship that just feels off. It's like decluttering a packed closet – let's tackle these things and make space for more good vibes in your life!

- Challenge the limits you've placed on yourself. Recall the last time you tried something new, like a complex recipe or a fresh hobby. It might have been uncomfortable initially, but the pride you felt afterwards is the joy of stepping outside your comfort zones. Push your thinking, question your usual choices, and explore fresh perspectives.

- Adapt gracefully to unexpected changes. How do you respond when plans fall apart? Being adaptable means you can adjust without losing your composure, maintaining calm amidst surprises.

- When you help others from the heart, you reveal a part of your true self. Remember the last time you assisted someone without expecting anything in return? That warm feeling is what genuine giving feels like. It reflects your core values and connects you deeply with others.

- Embrace a positive mindset, especially on tough days. Rather than fixating on the negatives, shift your focus to the positives. Finding joy in little things, such as a stunning sunset, can strengthen your identity and lift your mood.

- Discover what excites you, be it painting, writing, or gardening. When you engage in activities you love, your enthusiasm is infectious and truly shows who you are.

CONCLUSION:

Play to your strengths. Notice how fulfilling it feels to excel in an activity you're good at? When you focus on your abilities, life tends to flow more smoothly, allowing your true self to shine. Let's refine the content to adhere strictly to your style instructions, ensuring it's conversational, simple, and engaging without sounding like it was written by AI. Here's another attempt:

When you live your truth, you recognise and appreciate what makes you distinct. This means wearing what feels good, engaging in activities that spark joy, and speaking your thoughts freely, all without concern for others' judgements. This freedom is the heart of living authentically.

To go on this path, you first need to identify what truly matters to you, your core beliefs and values. Reflect on how these influence your daily interactions and career choices. It's about making a life that resonates with your deepest convictions.

At first, it can be scary to show the world who you really are. Finding what feels right takes time. You should focus on making steady progress rather than striving for perfection.

Ever feel like an outsider in your own circle due to your choices? This could be a sign that it's time to seek out a community that shares your passions and outlook.

The quest for authenticity affects both our personal and professional lives. We often find ourselves balancing our true identity, others' expectations, and what might seem like the safest path at the moment. Striking this balance demands patience and thoughtful decision-making.

The road to authenticity is rarely smooth. You may find yourself making hard choices, such as distancing from those who don't understand or accept you, embracing the risk of honesty in your conversations, or dealing with criticism. These are the steps necessary for letting your true self shine.

Living authentically is a profound journey that's not always easy. It may involve letting go of people who can't see you for who you are, taking chances by being genuine with others, and facing critique—all essential for revealing the real you.

THE JOURNEY AHEAD

As we reach the conclusion of our journey in *Lost at Forty* I reflect on the transformative paths we've explored together—paths that inspire a profound awakening to the dreams and desires that may have lain dormant as life unfolded in its busy cadence.

So far, we've discussed how authenticity, fulfilment, and bravery are required to align with our true selves. It's become clear that midlife is a rich opportunity to thrive and not a phase that we have to dread. Midlife is about progressing through life's chapters confidently and writing new ones with passion and purpose.

As we conclude, my hope is that the insights and strategies shared here have resonated with you and will inspire you to embrace this season of life with optimism and excitement. Midlife is indeed not a sunset, signalling the end of the day, but rather a second dawn, bright with promise and potential.

With a heart full of hope, I invite you now to take the lessons woven through these pages and use them as tools to carve out a life of richness and meaning. Remember, this book isn't merely a guide—it's a call to action to live deeply, boldly, and intentionally.

Let us shift our perspective together and see midlife not as a crisis but as a celebration of potential. Armed with the knowledge you now hold, you are more than capable of steering through this dynamic stage of life.

The strategies, stories, and heartfelt counsel contained in this book are yours to apply as you renew, rejuvenate, and redefine your existence.

As you move forward, embracing the coming years, keep in mind that life beyond forty is less about discovering who you are and more about creating who you wish to become. Your future doesn't unfold by fate but is crafted by the fearless decisions you make day by day. So, dream with vigour, challenge the status quo, and live with your whole heart.

In closing, let this book serve not just as a reflection of midlife's challenges but as a beacon of its myriad opportunities. May it be your companion on a journey filled with renewed dreams and exciting adventures. Thank you for walking this path with me. Together, let's step into our next chapters with excitement, embracing a midlife that is anything but limited. Here's to the dreams we will chase and the life we will shape—full of wonder, joy, and boundless discovery.

9 798889 556843